ECONOMIC DEVELOPMENT POLICIES

Publications in the Inner Cities Research Programme Series

1 Overview volume
Urban Economic Adjustment and the Future of British Cities: Directions for Urban Policy
Victor A. Hausner, Policy Studies Institute, London

2 Summary volume on five city studies
Urban Economic Change: Five City Studies
Members of the five research teams and the National Director

3 Bristol region study
Sunbelt City? A Study of Economic Change in Britain's M4 Growth Corridor
Martin Boddy, John Lovering, and Keith Bassett

4 Clydeside conurbation study
The City in Transition: Policies and Agencies for the Economic Regeneration of Clydeside
edited by W. F. Lever and Chris Moore

5 London metropolitan region study
The London Employment Problem
Nick Buck, Ian Gordon, and Ken Young, with John Ermisch and Liz Mills

6 West Midlands study
Crisis in the Industrial Heartland: A Study of the West Midlands
Ken Spencer, Andy Taylor, Barbara Smith, John Mawson, Norman Flynn, and Richard Batley

7 Newcastle metropolitan region study
Economic Development Policies: An Evaluative Study of the Newcastle Metropolitan Region
Fred Robinson, Colin Wren, John Goddard

8 Special research studies
Critical Issues in Urban Economic Development, vol. I
edited by Victor A. Hausner, Policy Studies Institute, London

9 Special research studies
Critical Issues in Urban Economic Development, vol. II
edited by Victor A. Hausner, Policy Studies Institute, London

10 Special research study
The New Economic Roles of UK Cities
Iain Begg and Barry Moore, Department of Applied Economics, University of Cambridge

11 Collective volume
Economic Change in British Cities
Members of the five research teams and the National Director

ECONOMIC DEVELOPMENT POLICIES

An Evaluative Study of the Newcastle Metropolitan Region

FRED ROBINSON
COLIN WREN
JOHN GODDARD

CLARENDON PRESS · OXFORD
1987

Oxford University Press, Walton Street, Oxford OX2 6DP
Oxford New York Toronto
Delhi Bombay Calcutta Madras Karachi
Petaling Jaya Singapore Hong Kong Tokyo
Nairobi Dar es Salaam Cape Town
Melbourne Auckland
and associated companies in
Beirut Berlin Ibadan Nicosia

Published in the United States
by Oxford University Press, New York

British Library Cataloguing in Publication Data
Robinson, Fred
Economic development policies : an evaluative study of the Newcastle metropolitan region.—(Inner cities research programme).
1. Newcastle-upon-Tyne (Tyne and Wear)—Industries 2. Newcastle-upon-Tyne (Tyne and Wear)—Economic conditions
I. Title II. Goddard, J.B. III. Wren, Colin IV. Series
338.9428'76 HC258.N/
ISBN 0–19–823271–3

Library of Congress Cataloging in Publication Data
Robinson, Fred.
Economic development policies.
(Inner cities research program)
1. Urban renewal—England—Newcastle upon Tyne Metropolitan Area (Tyne and Wear) 2. Urban policy—England—Newcastle upon Tyne Metropolitan Area (Tyne and Wear) 3. Newcastle upon Tyne Metropolitan Area (Tyne and Wear)—Economic conditions. 4. Subsidies—England—Newcastle upon Tyne Metropolitan Area (Tyne and Wear) I. Goddard, John B., 1943– . II. Wren, Colin. III. Title. IV. Series.
HT178.G72N487 1987 338.9428'76 87–12247
ISBN 0–19–8232713 (pbk.)

Set by Promenade Graphics
Printed in Great Britain
at the University Printing House, Oxford
by David Stanford
Printer to the University

FOREWORD

In 1982 the Environment and Planning Committee of the Economic and Social Research Council (SSRC at the time) initiated a three-year comparative research programme to examine inner city problems within the broad context of major structural and spatial changes occurring in Great Britain. The programme was developed by the then SSRC Inner Cities Working Party, chaired by Professor Peter Hall, and subsequently the Executive Panel on the Inner Cities, chaired by Professor Gordon Cameron. The proposal for the research was originally described in 'A Research Agenda' (chapter 8) of *The Inner City in Context* (ed. Peter Hall, Heinemann, 1981). The purpose of the programme was to examine the processes of urban change, the effects on urban socio-economic welfare, and the prospects, constraints, and requirements for more successful urban adjustment to structural change. The programme arose from concerns with the urban problems of economic decline, labour market imbalances, social distress, and the effectiveness of public policies in addressing these problems. It was hoped that the programme's findings would be useful for the improvement of public policies to strengthen urban economies (that is, foster growth, employment, and competitiveness), alleviate the distress caused by change, and improve the conditions of distressed inner city areas and deprived urban residents.

In practice, the overall programme focused on the economic aspects of urban change. Specifically, the programme sought to identify the key factors affecting urban economic change and to describe and explain the processes of local economic change. Secondly, it aimed to describe the consequences of change for the urban economy and the employment of its residents. Finally, the programme attempted to assess the effects of public policies on the process of change.

The programme was based on the idea that there is diversity in the economic performance of different urban and inner city areas in the UK and in their adjustment to external forces of change; for example, changes in business competition, technology, and residential patterns. A comparative examination of the nature, processes, and effects of economic change on different urban centres should help to clarify and explain the differences in the experiences of economic change among and within urban areas and to identify those factors (including public policies) which impede or facilitate urban and inner city adjustment to change: that is, economic growth, increased business competitiveness, employment generation, employment for the disadvantaged in urban labour markets, and the effectiveness of urban economic policies. The ESRC programme utilized a general framework of topics to assist individual urban studies and the comparative examination of urban economic change. The topics were: the changing nature of urban economic problems; the nature and causes of imbalances in urban labour markets; the unintended effects of central and local government policies on urban economic change, and the effectiveness of national and local urban economic policies; and the capabilities of local authorities to design and implement more effective economic development policies.

The Inner Cities Research Programme addressed these concerns through two avenues of work. The core of the programme was independent studies of four major urban centres of Great Britain which were selected by the SSRC as examples of the diversity of urban economic adjustment experiences: Glasgow and the Clydeside conurbation as an example of 'persistent economic decline'; Birmingham and the West Midlands conurbation as one of 'faltering growth'; the Bristol region as one of 'successful adaptation'; and two areas in London, one (Greenwich, Southwark, and Lewisham) exhibiting 'severe problems', the other (Brent, Ealing, and Hounslow) exemplifying more 'successful adaptation'. These were largely secondary research studies using existing data and analysing existing research. The studies were conducted by independent research teams with distinctive approaches and concerns, but linked by the overall programme's objectives and general framework of topical concerns, dialogue, information exchange, and some common data and analysis. The different research teams decided on the particular approach, subjects, and hypotheses which they considered most relevant to an understanding of economic change in their study areas; and critically examined the characterizations of those areas.

To these four initial studies a fifth study of the Newcastle metropolitan region was added, funded by the Department of the Environment, in order to broaden the sample of urban areas and focus particularly on an assessment of the relationship, impacts, and effectiveness of central and local government urban and regional economic development policies on an economically distressed city region that was a long-term recipient of government assistance.

In addition to these five core studies a number of smaller 'cross-cutting' studies were conducted by various researchers in order to provide a national statistical framework for the five city studies and uniform comparative data on the five city study areas, to examine in greater detail important aspects of urban economic change in a broader sample of urban areas, to explore the effects on change of important public policies, to provide a comparative international perspective, and to increase the general relevance of a case-study-based research programme. A list of the publications and their authors, resulting from all of these elements of the programme, appears at the beginning of this book.

In order to enhance the relevance of the research programme to public policy issues and communication with central government policy-makers, discussions were held with officials of three government agencies: the Department of the Enviroment, the Department of Trade and Industry, and the Manpower Services Commission. These agencies also assisted the programme through the provision of data, special analyses, and the co-operation of their regional offices. The individual city and cross-cutting studies involved extensive local contacts with government officials, representatives of business, labour and voluntary organizations, and other researchers and analysts.

The five city studies were conducted by members of research teams at the following institutions: the Department of Social and Economic Research at the University of Glasgow; the Institute of Local Government Studies and the Centre for Urban and Regional Studies at the University of Birmingham; the School for Advanced Urban Studies and the Department of Geography at the University of Bristol; the Policy Studies Institute in London and the Urban and Regional Studies Unit at the University of Kent; and the Centre for Urban and Regional Development Studies at the University of Newcastle upon Tyne.

Professor Brian Robson, former chairman of the ESRC Environment and Planning Committee, and Professor Noel Boaden and Paul McQuail, both then members of the Committee, advised on the implementation of the programme. They were assisted by Dr Angela Williams, Senior Scientific Officer to the Committee. Members of the former SSRC Executive Panel discussed, reviewed papers, and advised on the research during the course of the programme. The programme also benefited from the advice and comments of other urban analysts.

London 1985

VICTOR A. HAUSNER
Director, ESRC Inner Cities Research Programme

PREFACE

This study was commissioned by the Inner Cities Directorate of the Department of the Environment. It has also received support from the Economic and Social Research Council and forms part of the ESRC's Inner Cities Research Programme. The work was undertaken over the period January 1984 to December 1985 by the Centre for Urban and Regional Development Studies at the University of Newcastle upon Tyne.

We acknowledge the invaluable contributions of the other members of the research team: David Storey, John Howard, Fiona Waterhouse, and Elizabeth Holmes. David Storey helped with the initial formulation of the research strategy; John Howard and Elizabeth Holmes undertook work on labour market issues and spatial analyses of deprivation; and Fiona Waterhouse carried out reviews of local economic development policies and analysis of survey data. Geoff Hepworth provided considerable help with the survey of employees, and we owe a major debt of gratitude to our typist Denise Rainford for coping with numerous changes to the text. Officers of central and local government gave vital help by providing data and discussing policy, and we are grateful to the managers and employees of assisted firms who participated in our surveys. We would also like to thank members of the Steering Committee for their advice, support, and encouragement throughout this project. Michael Bach and Colin Packman of the Inner Cities Directorate of the Department of the Environment provided a great deal of assistance and proffered many useful comments. Finally, our thanks are due to Victor Hausner, National Director of the ESRC Inner Cities Research Programme and Brian Robson, former Chairman of the ESRC Environment and Planning Committee. The views expressed in this report are our own and not necessarily those of the Department of the Environment or of the Department of Trade and Industry.

Newcastle upon Tyne 1986

Fred Robinson
Colin Wren
John Goddard

CONTENTS

LIST OF FIGURES

LIST OF TABLES

ABBREVIATIONS

BSC(I)	British Steel Corporation (Industry) Ltd.
BTG	British Technology Group
CAT	City Action Team
CIA	Commercial Improvement Area
CoSIRA	Council for Small Industries in Rural Areas
CP	Community Programme
DHSS	Department of Health and Social Security
D.o.E.	Department of the Environment
DTI	Department of Trade and Industry
ECSC	European Coal and Steel Community
ENTRUST	Tyne and Wear Enterprise Trust
ERDF	European Regional Development Fund
ESF	European Social Fund
ESRC	Economic and Social Research Council
IAP	Inner Area Programme
IIA	Industrial Improvement Area
JURUE	Joint Unit for Research on the Urban Environment
MLH	Minimum List Heading
MSC	Manpower Services Commission
NDC	Northern Development Company
NECCA	North-East County Councils Association
NEDC	North of England Development Council
NEI	Northern Engineering Industries PLC
NRST	Northern Region Strategy Team
NSA	National Selective Assistance
PSMRU	Public Sector Management Research Unit
RDG	Regional Development Grant
RSA	Regional Selective Assistance
RTPI	Royal Town Planning Institute
SAUS	School for Advanced Urban Studies
SDA	Special Development Area
SENET	South-East Northumberland Enterprise Trust

SIC	Standard Industrial Classification
UDG	Urban Development Grant
YTS	Youth Training Scheme

1

Introduction

Newcastle upon Tyne was one of the key centres of the Industrial Revolution. At the beginning of the nineteenth century it was at the heart of the thriving and rapidly expanding Great Northern Coalfield and by the end of the century had become an acknowledged world leader in shipbuilding and heavy engineering. But this dependence on a few heavy industries was subsequently to prove a major liability—a point clearly demonstrated by the severe impact of the Depression during the 1920s and 1930s. Since then, there have been periods of relative prosperity, but the underlying, long-term trend has been one of economic decline, centred on the gradual disappearance of those traditional industries that were the basis for the area's industrialization.

As one of the first areas to experience the process of industrial decline, Tyneside was also one of the earliest beneficiaries of Government regional policy intervention. The Team Valley Trading Estate, set up in the 1930s, is a well-known example of these early regional policy efforts. Regional policy was vigorously pursued by the Government just after the war, essentially abandoned in the 1950s, and then reintroduced in the early 1960s and has been applied with varying degrees of enthusiasm since then. For half a century, the Newcastle area (and most of the North-East) has been subject to regional policy aid—and has, indeed, been seen as a textbook example illustrating economic decline and public policy response.

Since the mid-1970s a number of other economic development initiatives and agencies have been established alongside conventional regional policy measures. There has been a substantial growth in local initiatives, including a major increase in local authority involvement in economic development and the emergence of a number of new locally based agencies mainly concerned with the support of small firms. Central government policy has undergone some important changes, notably a shift in policy attention from 'regional' to 'urban' issues, and the associated growth of the Urban Programme. In addition, economic development policy has also been supported by the creation and expansion of the Manpower Services Commission (MSC) and resources from the European Community's Regional and Social Funds. The Newcastle area is a kind of 'policy laboratory', a good place to assess the successes and failures of different policies. In particular, the area is subject to both regional and urban policy, providing the opportunity to compare and contrast these differing conceptions of the 'problem' and the 'solution'.

This study is primarily an exercise in policy evaluation, examining, in detail, the impacts and effectiveness of policy measures concerned with the provision of *direct financial assistance to industry* in the metropolitan region centred on Newcastle. Like the other city case-studies in the ESRC programme, we have sought to offer a general view of economic problems and responses to them, but this study is much more sharply focused on the effects of specific policy instruments. This particularly reflects the concerns of the Department of the Environment; this study was commissioned by the Department as part of its programme of research evaluating economic projects within the Urban Programme. In addition, the inclusion of this research as one of the city studies ensured that the ESRC programme would address practical and specific questions of policy design and implementation.

The provision of financial assistance—usually in the form of loans or grants to firms—has represented one of the key measures in economic development policy. Thus, the main feature of regional policy, administered by the Department of Trade and Industry (DTI), is a system of cash subsidies to firms in the Assisted Areas. Most local authorities operate loans and grants schemes to help firms, while public sector provision of industrial premises often involves rent subsidies. Such inducements represent considerable public expenditure, but surprisingly little is known about its distribution, and even less is known about its effects.

This research attempts to establish the pattern of assistance expenditure in the Newcastle metropolitan region, providing the opportunity—for the first time—to comprehensively examine the distribution of assistance from several agencies within a specific area. The study has investigated the impact of financial assistance on the operation of firms (investment, efficiency, competitiveness, etc.), on their employment (job creation, retention, or loss), and the consequent labour market effects (in particular, the spatial distribution of employees of the assisted firms). With reference to the concerns of urban policy, the research has sought to determine how far policies targeted on firms in the inner areas of the conurbation benefit inner area residents. We consider how far assistance policies have responded to the economic problems of the area, examining the extent to which these policies have served to fulfil industrial objectives at the firm level, such as restructuring and increasing competitiveness, and served to generate employment. The research is intended to establish how these economic development policies might be made more effective, viewing this in terms of the differing roles and contributions which may be made by the different approaches and also with regard to the ways in which policies are implemented and delivered.

The study has been strongly based on empirical research and is therefore firmly rooted in the practical application of policy. A number of complementary approaches were adopted to establish the impacts of financial assistance.

Firstly, interviews were conducted with members of agencies operating economic development policy measures in the study area. These were used to establish the range of policies being pursued, their evolution, objectives, methods of implementation, and the resources involved. Secondly, agencies providing direct financial assistance to firms were asked to supply detailed data on individual cases of assistance over the period 1974–84. Basic information on nearly 2500 assisted establishments was assembled. Thirdly, managers at 201 of these assisted establishments participated in a detailed questionnaire survey, which focused on the impact of assisted projects on the operation and employment of these firms. Finally, to explore the effects of these assistance measures on the labour market, a questionnaire survey of employees at 120 assisted establishments was conducted. This was used to determine how the benefits of employment are distributed within the labour market, and was supplemented by an analysis of Census travel-to-work data.

This research represents a contribution to methodological development; we believe that the methods of economic policy evaluation formulated and tested in this study could usefully be employed in further evaluative work in this field. The evaluation of economic development policies is difficult and time-consuming—an indication of this is the amount of effort involved in this study. Here it is worth noting that financial assistance measures are probably more amenable to evaluation than many other forms of economic development policy (such as the provision of premises, environmental improvements, and the provision of advisory services). It should also be pointed out that evaluation ought to be a continuing process, comprising monitoring and assessment, and that this should be directly linked to policy revision.

The study begins with a discussion of the essential characteristics of the Newcastle metropolitan region, summarizing its development and indicating its particular economic problems (Chapter 2). This is followed, in Chapter 3, by an examination of public policy responses to these problems since the mid-1970s. Chapter 4 looks in detail at direct financial assistance to firms, beginning with an analysis of the scale and incidence of assistance expenditure. In Chapter 5 we draw on the findings of the surveys, to assess the impact of these measures on the performance and employment of assisted establishments. Finally, bringing this material together, Chapter 6 considers how effective assistance has been in helping to tackle the area's problems and looks at some of the ways in which policy could be improved.

2

Economic Change in the Newcastle Metropolitan Region

This chapter briefly examines the changing economic structure of the Newcastle metropolitan region, focusing especially on the last decade. It describes the pattern of long-term decline and highlights the basic structural characteristics of the economy which have helped to generate or reinforce its current problems.

The Newcastle Metropolitan Region

The study area, the *Newcastle metropolitan region*, has been defined with respect to labour market relationships and the application of regional policy. It comprises the 'functional region' (Coombes *et al.*, 1980, 1981) centred on Newcastle upon Tyne and includes the conurbation's commuting hinterland and covers those areas consistently subject to regional policy over the period 1971–84. The functional region concept has the advantage of defining an area which recognizes the interdependencies of an urban core and the surrounding settlements, providing a framework for examining a 'local economy'. It recognizes, in particular, the interrelationships of the local labour market and also provides a diversity of economic structures and policy environments for comparative analysis.

This functional region does not constitute a single administrative entity; it is composed of eleven local authority Districts and incorporates the whole of the Metropolitan County of Tyne and Wear and parts of Northumberland and Durham (Figure 2.1). The main service centres within the Tyne and Wear conurbation are Newcastle itself, Sunderland, Gateshead, North and South Shields, and Washington New Town. Outside Tyne and Wear County there are extensive rural areas but also a number of subordinate centres, such as Durham to the south and Morpeth to the north and the local authority sponsored new town of Cramlington in Northumberland. The south-western part of the study area includes Consett, in Derwentside District, which experienced a major steel closure in 1980, while the eastern part of the area contains six collieries on the active periphery of the coalfield. The population of the Newcastle metropolitan region is 1.56 million (1981), and Tyne and Wear County, with a population of 1.14 million accounts for nearly three-quarters of this total.

Many of the area's economic problems are long-standing and their origins can be traced back to the nature and pattern of industrialization in the nine-

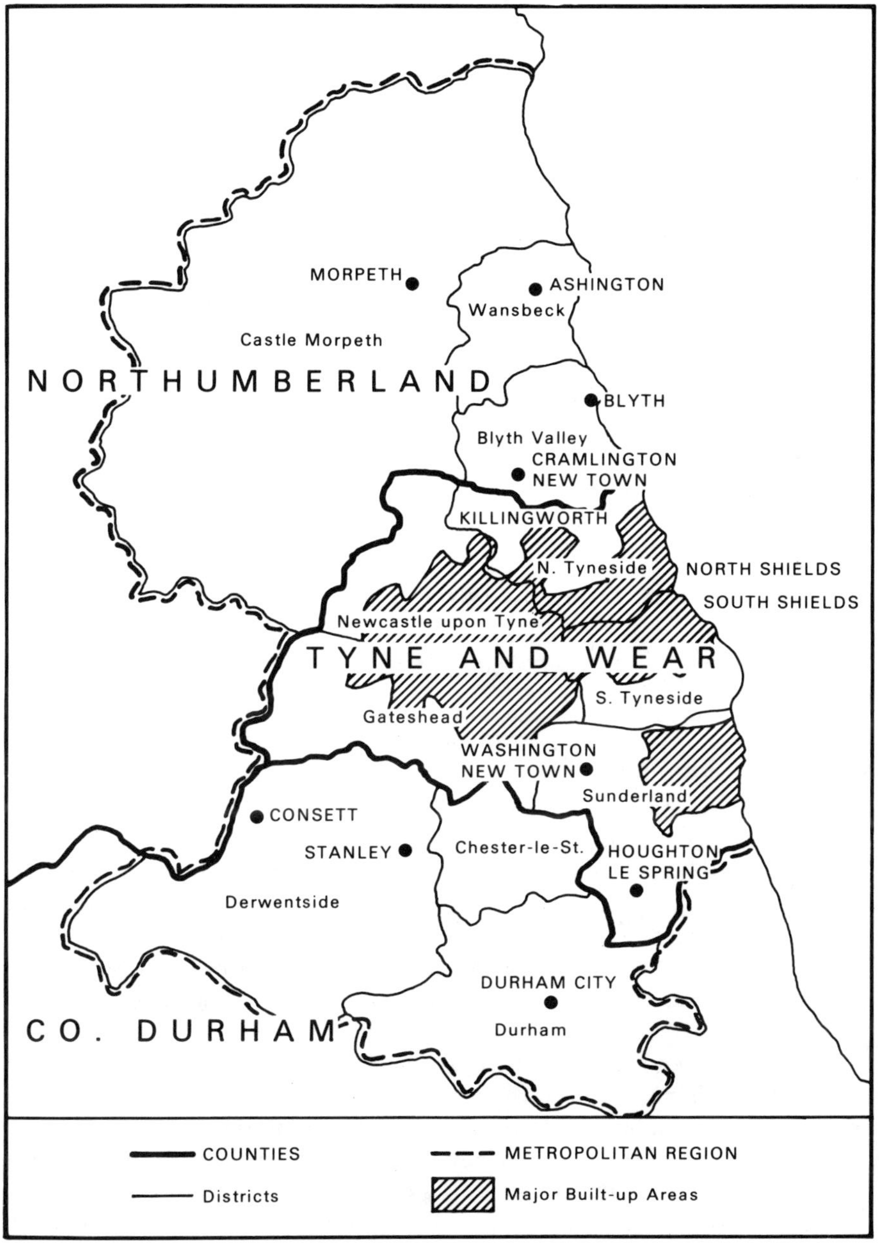

Fig. 2.1. The Newcastle metropolitan region.

teenth century. The area has long been identified as a 'distressed', 'depressed', or 'problem' region (or, more euphemistically, 'less prosperous' or 'less favoured'), and has a history of regional policy intervention which stretches back more than fifty years. It has been described as 'a museum piece of the former glories of industrial Britain', and a 'laboratory for regional development policies' (House, 1969, p. 15). More recently, there has been a shift of attention towards 'urban' problems and locally administered policy responses. All the Districts in Tyne and Wear have been designated for assistance under the 1978 Inner Urban Areas Act (which was based on the innovative locally promoted Tyne and Wear Act, 1976). Although the primary focus of our research has been on the period 1974–84, the next section of this chapter considers the antecedents to the area's problems and past responses to them—not least because the long history of industrial decline and the sequence of policy initiatives and related agencies, laid one upon the other, have in many senses also become part of the contemporary problems of the area.

Historical Context: Economic Development and Regional Policy

Industrialization

The basis for the industrialization of the Newcastle metropolitan region was coal-mining, which developed initially along the banks of the rivers Tyne and Wear. As early as 1600, nearly 250 000 tons of coal was exported annually from the Tyne to the London market and this trade contributed to the development of Newcastle as a commercial centre and as a port. The availability of coal also stimulated some early local industrial activity, including the production of alkali, glass, and pottery—industries which saw considerable expansion in the first half of the nineteenth century and then declined to insignificance. From the late eighteenth century onwards, coal became an increasingly significant, ultimately dominant, element of the area's economy. By the late 1820s two million tons of coal a year was shipped from the Tyne, a figure which doubled over the next twenty years. Mining activity moved into areas further away from the rivers, a process made feasible first by the construction of wagonways from the new collieries to the riverside and then extended by the development of railways to carry coal to the ports. Innovations in mining technology, notably steam pumps, also allowed the sinking of deeper and more productive pits. Coal-mining provided the impetus for the area's economic development, fostering the growth of shipbuilding, the local invention of railways, and the development of steam engines and mechanical engineering (McCord, 1979).

The second half of the nineteenth century witnessed an enormous increase in industrial activity in the region; there was 'a general euphoria, a heady feeling that this was the greatest and most progressive corner of the world' (Bean, 1971, p. 93). A further, major expansion of coal-mining took place, extending across much of County Durham and south-east Northumberland and involving a substantial increase in the export trade. By 1900, nearly 15 million tons of coal a year was shipped from the Tyne. This period saw the development of manufacturing industry on a large scale with the buildup of shipbuilding and heavy engineering industries along the banks of the Tyne and Wear. Iron- and steel-making was now primarily centred on the works at Consett which, by the 1880s, was producing 10 per cent of UK steel. The population more than doubled between 1850 and 1900 and this stimulated rapid but inadequate urban development which gave rise to overcrowding, and public health and social problems.

The shipyards on the Tyne and Wear successfully switched to iron construction from the 1850s and established a lead position in world markets based on innovation, scale, and influence. By the 1890s, these yards accounted for three-quarters of tonnage being built in the UK. Associated industries such as ship repair and marine engineering shared in this booming market. In the west end of Newcastle, armaments and warship manufacture became the dominant industries and by the turn of the century Armstrong's works employed over 25 000. Other engineering industries also developed, in particular the Parsons' works manufacturing turbines both for ship propulsion and electricity generation. A notable feature of this period was the concentration of power and wealth; a small number of families and individuals played a vital role in the area's economic, social, and political development. Some were landed aristocrat coal-owners (the Lambton and Londonderry families, for example), while others were self-made magnates, generally of middle-class origins (Armstrong, Palmer, Parsons). Their interests were extensive, ranging from coal to manufacturing, to shipping, to banking, and they actively participated in managing these industries and also played an important part in the region's public affairs.

Depression, rearmament, reconstruction

As industrial expansion had accelerated so the industrial structure narrowed: skills, enterprise, and capital were concentrated in the staple industries of coal, shipbuilding, and heavy engineering (Mess, 1928, p. 23). This narrow base proved vulnerable to foreign competition and was heavily dependent on continuing high demand for armaments. Tyneside became a 'huge arsenal and dockyard' during the First World War, but once the post-war boom subsided it was plunged into severe depression, which marked the beginning of a long (and continuing) period of decline. Armstrong's, in difficulty before the war and revived through rearmament, had to be rescued by amalgamation with Vickers in 1927. Palmer's naval yard at Jarrow was closed down completely in an effort to cut capacity in the industry, plunging the company town of Jarrow into severe crisis (Wilkinson, 1939). Merchant yards also suffered large reductions in demand during the Depression, as did companies in marine engineering. Coal-mining was hard hit by falling demand in both domestic and overseas markets, aggravated by increasing competition from foreign producers.

Throughout the inter-war years unemployment was high, especially in the shipbuilding towns and the West Durham pit villages. In the North-East as a whole, the official unemployment rate was 28.5 per cent by 1932, twice the rate for the South-East (Middleton, 1985, p. 22). One response was migration: Jarrow's population fell by 37 per cent between 1921 and 1939, Hebburn lost 25 per cent, and South Shields 21 per cent.

Government intervention to ameliorate regional unemployment began in 1928 with industrial transference schemes to promote increased migration, but the impact was limited not least because of the shortage of jobs elsewhere. It was also recognized that selective migration could undermine the viability of areas losing population (Odber, 1965, pp. 332–3). The 1934 Special Areas Act marked the first, tentative efforts towards helping the 'depressed areas' directly, initially through infrastructure projects and then through the development of industrial ('Trading') estates and factories to rent, followed in 1937 with the provision of loans and grants to incoming industry (Pitfield, 1978). Tyneside, Wearside, and County Durham were designated as 'Special Areas', but the effect of these policies before the War was limited. The first industrial estate was started at Team Valley in Gateshead in 1936, but this and other new estates in the area together employed only about 2500 workers by 1939. It was rearmament and the production imperatives of wartime which restored the economy, again 'expanding the basic industries which had caused so much inter-war unemployment' (Pepler and MacFarlane, 1949, p. 43).

The development of wartime planning and the rise of 'labourism' and 'welfarism', allied to the demands of reconstruction, secured a place for regional policy after the War. Most of the study area was designated as part of the North-East Development Area under the 1945 Distribution of Industry Act, which provided for the construction of estates and factories in the Development Areas while restricting factory building elsewhere. After early successes—because of the high demand for factory space—the policy weakened after the Balance of Payments crisis in 1947 and was then in abeyance from 1951 to 1958. However, by 1952 twenty industrial estates had been built in the study area, providing over 26 000 jobs in 184 factories. The majority of these jobs were in newer, lighter industries, such as textiles, electrical goods, clothing, and light engineering. Half the work-force in these new factories comprised women, thus sustaining the growth in female economic activity begun during the War.

The 1950s and 1960s

Throughout the 1950s the area experienced low levels of unemployment (2 per cent to 4 per cent), owing to strong demand in the staple industries, especially coal and steel. However, falling demand in shipbuilding (attributable largely to foreign competition) and the commencement of pit closures (mainly as a result of competition from cheap oil) raised unemployment and led to the revival of regional policy at the end of the decade. Initially, south-east Tyneside and Wearside were designated as Development Districts under the 1960 Local Employment Act. At first the approach was to designate unemployment 'blackspots' (generally areas with unemployment above $4\frac{1}{2}$ per cent), but as conditions deteriorated coverage was extended to include almost all the study area by 1963. Again, the main thrust of policy was industrial estate development, but financial assistance became more important after the introduction of a standard grant system in 1963. The principal aim was to stimulate the movement of branch plants into the area and thus provide new sources of employment.

The period from 1963 to the early 1970s was one of major economic change in the North-East, which included a large-scale reduction in mining, active regional policy, service sector growth, and infrastructure renewal. The appointment of Lord Hailsham in 1963 as Minister with special responsibility for the North-East resulted in the preparation of a co-ordinated programme of action, led by central government, to diversify and modernize the region, underpinned by 'accelerated investment in public services'—notably roads, factories, and industrial estates, but also including town centre redevelopment, housing, and land reclamation. The 'Hailsham Plan' (Cmnd. 2206) recommended the establishment of a new town at Washington (designated in 1964) and included most of the study area as part of a regional 'growth zone' within which economic development efforts were to be concentrated. Following Hailsham, regional policy and planning was continued and developed by the 1964–70 Labour Government with expenditure rising from £80 million in 1966/7 to £259 million in 1968/9 (Manners *et al.*, 1972, p. 51). The whole of the study area (indeed, the whole of the Northern Region) was designated a 'Development Area' under the 1966 Industrial Development Act, although the 'blackspot' approach was reintroduced in 1967 by the designation of 'Special Development Areas' offering a higher level of financial assistance. The five SDAs in the area covered the pit-closure areas of north-west Durham and south-east Northumberland, but Tyneside and Wearside were added in 1971. The traditional instruments of regional policy—factories and financial aid—were used, the latter including not only (increased) grants for investment, but also a wages subsidy (Regional Employment Premium, introduced in 1967, abolished in 1977).

The changing industrial structure of the area between 1961 and 1971 is shown in Table 2.1. Over this period, *coal-mining* experienced massive decline, with a reduction of nearly 60 000 jobs (Hudson, 1985). *Manufacturing* experienced relatively little overall decline (−4.4 per cent) with similar rates of loss of male (−4.1 per cent) and female employment (−5.3 per cent) and small changes in most industries apart from shipbuilding (which lost over 16 000 jobs, a fall of 34.9 per cent). The movement of *branch plants* into the area, supported by active regional policy, helped to sustain, diversify, and restructure manufacturing and so compensate for job losses within this sector. It has been estimated that this movement of industry generated just under 38 000 new jobs in the Northern Region as a whole over the period 1961–71 (NRST, 1977, p. 48). But the major element of change was *service sector* growth, especially in *public sector services*, such as health and education (SIC 25) and public administration (SIC 27). It was this which *numerically* offset the losses in coal-mining—although the typically much higher proportion of females in service sector occupations meant that there was, nevertheless, a significant decline in male employment over the decade. Female employment grew both in absolute terms and as a proportion of total employment; by 1971 37.5 per cent of employees were women, compared with 31.3 per cent in 1961. *Total employment fell by only 3.3 per cent between 1961 and 1971* despite huge losses in mining, but it was not so much regional policy which 'delivered' jobs—rather, it was the expansion of public expenditure on services.

While the formal emphasis of public policy during this period was on the North-East Region as a whole, a major part of the impact of industrial change and policy was within the Newcastle metropolitan region as defined for this study. A majority of the region's job losses in mining and shipbuilding occurred within the broadly defined labour market area of the Newcastle metropolitan region, while other parts of the North-East, notably Teesside, were relatively prosperous. Although not conceived in urban policy terms, many of the regional policy initiatives of this period significantly influenced the development of the conurbation (the designation of Washington New Town, for example). In addition, expansion of the service sector, especially public services, together with extensive city centre renewal, served to strengthen Newcastle itself as a regional capital.

Economic Change in the 1970s and 1980s

The performance of the local economy, 1971–1978

The period up to the mid-1970s represented, in many respects, a continuation of the perspectives and policies established at the time of the Hailsham Report: 'modernization', diversification through branch plant operations, and service sector development. Total employment grew by 2.6 per cent over the period 1971–8 because further service sector growth was more than suf-

Table 2.1(a). *Employment Change in the Newcastle Metropolitan Region by Industrial Order, 1961–1981*

Industrial order (1968 SIC)	Total Employment ('000s)				% Change in Employment		
	1961	1971	1978	1981	1961–71	1971–78	1978–81
1 Agriculture, forestry, fishing	5.0	3.4	2.7	2.4	−33.2	−19.3	−12.9
2 Mining & quarrying	97.1	38.2	28.6	22.6	−60.6	−25.1	−21.0
TOTAL PRIMARY	102.1	41.6	31.4	25.0	−59.3	−24.6	−20.3
3 Food, drink, & tobacco	19.1	18.9	14.5	12.1	−0.9	−23.0	−16.5
4 Coal & petroleum products	2.1	1.5	1.6	1.4	−25.5	+3.1	−12.6
5 Chemicals & allied industries	11.9	12.6	10.4	9.2	+5.5	−17.3	−11.2
6 Metal manufacture	13.4	11.4	12.0	5.3	−15.1	+5.5	−55.7
7 Mechanical engineering	39.5	39.6	36.2	26.2	+0.3	−8.6	−27.8
8 Instrument engineering	0.7	2.2	2.6	2.3	+200.3	+16.6	−11.0
9 Electrical engineering	28.3	34.1	27.3	21.7	+20.5	−19.8	−20.6
10 Shipbuilding & marine engineering	47.8	31.1	29.5	23.1	−34.9	−5.3	−21.5
11 Vehicles	3.5	3.4	3.1	2.4	−2.9	−8.4	−21.9
12 Metal goods n.e.s.	6.3	6.5	7.7	5.2	+3.7	+19.2	−33.2
13 Textiles	3.8	6.4	5.7	4.6	+67.1	−9.9	−18.9
14 Leather, leather goods, & fur	1.0	0.9	0.4	0.2	−12.6	−54.1	−39.5
15 Clothing & footwear	16.8	15.7	13.2	8.3	−6.4	−15.7	−37.0
16 Bricks, pottery, glass, & cement	11.3	10.0	8.3	6.9	−11.3	−17.3	−16.8
17 Timber, furniture, etc.	7.3	5.8	5.5	5.4	−20.9	−5.0	−1.1
18 Paper, printing, & publishing	9.5	10.0	11.8	11.5	+5.3	+18.1	−2.4
19 Other manufacturing	7.7	9.7	9.9	8.1	+26.1	+1.7	−18.3
TOTAL MANUFACTURING	229.9	219.7	199.7	154.1	−4.4	−9.1	−22.9
20 TOTAL CONSTRUCTION	43.6	43.1	42.3	33.7	−1.2	−1.8	−20.4
21 Gas, electricity, & water	10.9	12.7	12.1	11.5	+16.4	−4.2	−5.3
22 Transport & communication	41.1	35.8	33.7	31.2	−12.8	−6.0	−7.5
23 Distributive trades	82.5	76.7	80.7	75.2	−7.0	+5.1	−6.8
24 Insurance, banking, etc.	9.3	16.0	20.1	24.9	+62.6	+25.7	+24.3
25 Professional & scientific services	53.4	81.5	100.2	91.9	+52.6	+23.0	−8.3
26 Miscellaneous services	48.2	54.9	67.9	69.4	+13.9	+23.7	+2.2
27 Public administration[b]	26.3	44.9	54.7	49.2	+70.7	+21.8	−10.1
TOTAL SERVICES	272.3	322.5	369.4	353.3	+18.4	+14.6	−4.4
TOTAL ALL ORDERS	647.9	626.9	642.9	566.1	−3.3	+2.6	−11.9

[a] 1961 data converted from the 1958 SIC by MLH disaggregation of 1958 order 4 (Chemicals, etc.) into 1968 orders 4 and 5; and 1958 order 6 (Engineering and Electrical Goods) into 1968 orders 7, 8, and 9.

[b] 1961 figure does not include civil servants.

Source: Manpower Services Commission; Annual Census of Employment.

Table 2.1(b). *Male and Female Employment Change in the Newcastle Metropolitan Region by Industrial Sector, 1961–1981*

Industrial sectors (orders)		Male Employment ('000s)				% Change in Employment		
		1961[a]	1971	1978	1981	1961–71	1971–78	1978–81
1–2	Primary	98.8	39.7	29.9	23.7	−59.8	−24.8	−20.7
3–19	Manufacturing	166.6	159.8	148.1	115.3	−4.1	−7.3	−22.2
20	Construction	41.6	41.0	39.8	31.0	−1.5	−3.0	−22.1
21–27	Services[b]	138.2	151.1	161.1	153.8	+9.4	+6.6	−4.5
TOTAL		445.3	391.6	378.9	323.7	−12.0	−3.3	−14.6
Industrial Sectors (orders)		Female Employment ('000s)				% Change in Employment		
		1961[a]	1971	1978	1981	1961–71	1971–78	1978–81
1–2	Primary	3.3	1.9	1.5	1.3	−42.8	−20.9	−10.5
3–19	Manufacturing	63.3	59.9	51.6	38.8	−5.3	−13.9	−24.8
20	Construction	2.0	2.1	2.5	2.7	+4.0	+20.7	+5.9
21–27	Services[b]	134.1	171.3	208.4	199.5	+27.8	+21.6	−4.2
TOTAL		202.7	235.2	264.0	242.3	+16.1	+12.2	−8.2

[a] 1961 data converted from the 1958 SIC by MLH disaggregation of 1958 order 4 (Chemicals, etc.) into 1968 orders 4 and 5; and 1958 order 6 (Engineering and Electrical Goods) into 1968 orders 7, 8, and 9.

[b] 1961 figure does not include civil servants.

Source: Manpower Services Commission; Annual Census of Employment.

ficient to compensate for continuing losses in manufacturing and mining. Manufacturing employment declined by 9.1 per cent over this period, largely owing to reductions in the engineering industries, but this was, in fact, a rate of decline less than that for Great Britain as a whole (−14.3 per cent) even despite the structural characteristics of the area's economy. Undoubtedly regional policy helped to slow the rate of manufacturing job loss by supporting investment in some existing industries and attracting branch plants; in 1978, 9.9 per cent of manufacturing jobs in Tyne and Wear were at relocated or branch plant operations which had opened in the area since 1965 (Tyne and Wear County Council, 1982). Job losses in mining over this period were smaller than over the previous decade since so much employment had already disappeared. As in the 1960s, strong growth in public sector services—and also some private services, such as insurance and banking—largely generated female employment (much of which was part-time) while losses in mining and manufacturing had a considerable impact on male employment. By 1978, only 31.1 per cent of jobs in the area were in manufacturing industry and only 4.5 per cent in mining. 41.1 per cent of employees were women. The area had undergone significant economic 'adjustment' and it was said to have 'successfully initiated a far-reaching process of restructuring and modernization' (NRST, 1977, p. 100).

Employment trends may be further examined through shift-share analysis, which provides a comparison between *actual* employment change and the change which would be *expected* if the local economy had followed national employment trends. Table 2.2 shows that, over the period 1971–8, the Newcastle metropolitan region had an overall employment growth of 0.4 per cent greater than would have been 'expected', given its industrial structure. This is seen to be accounted for by the contribution of public service sector growth which provided more than 9000 jobs over and above that which would be expected had employment changed in line with national trends. The major differential loss, to offset these 'extra' jobs in public services, was in primary industries. Manufacturing performed about the same as 'expected' in relation to the national pattern of decline in those industries which made up the industrial structure of the study area. Overall, it appears that the economy performed relatively well in this period due to the expansion of public sector services and, to some extent, as a result of support provided to manufacturing industries through regional policy measures. This relatively *good performance* is further demonstrated by comparing the five metropolitan regions of the ESRC case-studies: only Bristol and Newcastle experienced an increase in total employment and they also both performed better than 'expected'. But, in spite of this, unemployment represented an increasingly serious problem, both because service sector growth had not compensated for the *kinds* of jobs lost in the staple industries and also because the labour force was increasing as a consequence of demographic trends and higher rates of female participation. Unemployment in the study area nearly doubled from 4.9 per cent in 1973 to 9.6 per cent at June 1979.

Recession and job loss, 1978–1986

Economic conditions deteriorated dramatically from 1978–79, with especially severe and serious consequences for the North (NECCA, 1986). Between 1978 and 1981, total employment in the area fell by 11.8 per cent. This decline has since continued and further job losses, largely in traditional manufacturing industries and in coal-mining, are expected (Tyne and Wear County Council, 1985a). Almost every industry experienced job losses, but the strongest impact was in *manufacturing and male employment. In only three years, manufacturing employment fell by 22.9 per cent* and by 1981 accounted for only 27.2 per cent of all jobs in the study area. The heavy traditional industries suffered the largest job losses, reflecting the long-term problems of lack of competitiveness and overseas competition, compounded by falling demand in conditions of recession. But the newer, lighter manufacturing industries have also been affected.

Table 2.2. *Shift-share Analysis of Employment Trends, 1971–1978*

Metropolitan regions	Employment				National and structural components			Differential component	% differential
	June 1971	June 1978	Change in employment	% change	National	Structural	% structural		
Bristol	410 620	428 032	−17 412	4.2	11 167	2 042	0.5	4 202	1.0
Glasgow	820 169	789 976	−30 193	−3.7	22 305	−4 040	−0.5	−48 458	−5.9
London	5 758 784	5 664 535	−94 249	−1.6	156 615	197 290	3.4	−448 154	−7.8
Newcastle	626 867	642 869	16 002	2.6	17 048	−3 787	−0.6	2 740	0.4
West Midlands	1 337 975	1 327 369	−10 606	−0.8	36 387	−24 389	−1.8	−22 604	−1.7
Newcastle region									
Industrial sectors									
Primary	41 579	31 351	−10 228	−24.6	1 131	−7 165	−17.2	−4 194	−10.1
Manufacturing	219 692	199 746	−19 946	−9.1	5 975	−25 184	−11.5	−737	−0.3
Construction	43 110	42 236	−784	−1.8	1 172	−1 195	−2.8	−761	−1.8
Public services	155 807	180 473	24 666	15.8	4 237	11 175	7.2	9 254	5.9
Private services	166 679	188 973	22 294	13.4	4 533	18 582	11.1	−821	−0.5

Source: Annual Census of Employment.

Analysis of employment change A 'components of change' analysis of manufacturing industry in Tyne and Wear provides some indications of the scale and significance of the different elements contributing to recent employment change (Tyne and Wear County Council, 1986). The number of manufacturing jobs in the County fell by more than a quarter between 1976 and 1981, a decline of 45 637. This *net* loss was made up as follows:

			(surviving plants)		
Total mfg employment in Tyne & Wear, 1981 (est.)	= Total mfg employment in Tyne & Wear, 1976	+ openings	+ expansions	− contractions	− closures
126 271	= 171 908	+ 4 525	+ 10 913	− 34 991	− 26 084
Net change	= −45 637				

In this period, dominated by the recession from 1979, contractions and closures were the major components, together accounting for gross losses of over 61 000 jobs. Gross gains amounted to only 15 000 jobs, only one-third of which came from the opening of new plants. The rapid acceleration in gross job losses was the main reason why Tyne and Wear employment fell much faster in this period than in the early 1970s since the annual rate of total gross gains actually changed little. The contribution of new openings to this total did, however, decline significantly (Tyne and Wear County Council, 1986, p. 2), reflecting the considerable reduction in branch plant movement into the area in conditions of recession.

Shift-share analysis on employment data for all sectors and encompassing the whole study area shows that the Newcastle metropolitan region performed particularly badly during the period 1978–81. This analysis revealed that the area had suffered a 6.5 per cent decline of employment over and beyond that which would be 'expected' if the area's industries had followed the national trend, and indicated that its employment performance was considerably worse than that of the other case-study metropolitan regions (Table 2.3). Of the 41 600 'extra' jobs lost during this period (the 'differential component'), 14 600 were in manufacturing, 3700 and 5200 respectively in the primary and construction sectors, and 7400 in private services, while the previously buoyant public services sector showed a net 'deficit' of over 10 600 jobs. Clearly, the policies pursued during the previous decade had not succeeded in creating a strong private sector economy that was capable of withstanding national recession, while public expenditure reductions checked the growth in service employment which previously had compensated (at least numerically) for the decline of manufacturing jobs.

Job-shedding by major employers One of the main features of recent economic change has been job-shedding by the major companies, in the newer as well

Table 2.3. *Shift-share Analysis of Employment Trends, 1978–1981*

Metropolitan regions	Employment				National and structural components			Differential component	% differential
	June 1978	June 1981	Change in employment	% change	National	Structural	% structural		
Bristol	428 032	414 972	−13 060	−3.1	−21 845	12 679	3.0	−3 894	−0.9
Glasgow	789 976	712 319	−77 657	−9.8	−40 316	−5 073	−0.6	−32 268	−4.1
London	5 664 535	5 521 874	−142 661	−2.5	−289 090	170 096	+3.0	−23 667	−0.4
Newcastle	642 869	566 720	−76 149	−11.8	−32 809	−1 772	−0.3	−41 568	−6.5
West Midlands	1 327 369	1 193 231	−134 138	−10.1	−67 743	−60 772	−4.5	−5 623	−0.4
Newcastle region									
Industrial sectors									
Primary	31 351	25 000	−6 351	−20.3	−1 600	−1 025	−3.3	−3 726	−11.9
Manufacturing	199 746	154 071	−45 675	−22.9	−10 194	−20 851	−10.4	−14 630	−7.3
Construction	42 326	33 691	−8 635	−20.4	−2 160	−1 239	−2.9	−5 236	−12.4
Public services	180 473	165 356	−15 117	−8.4	−9 211	4 652	2.6	−10 559	−5.9
Private services	188 973	188 602	−371	−0.2	−9 644	16 691	8.8	−7 417	−3.9

Source: Annual Census of Employment.

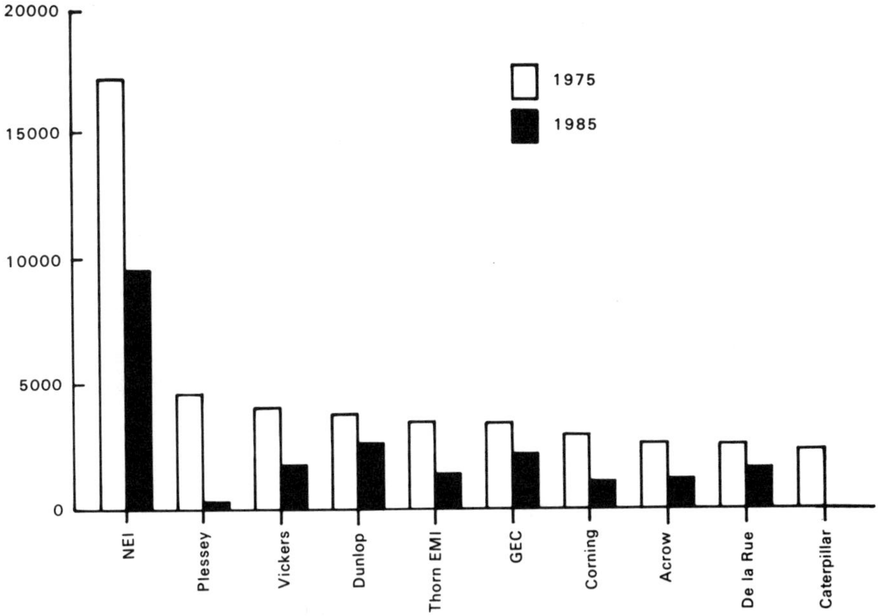

Fig. 2.2. Employment change in the top ten private manufacturing companies in Tyne & Wear, 1975–1985.

Source: N. E. Trade Union Studies Information Unit (1985), Figure 17, 26.

as in the traditional industries, and in both the private and public sectors. In Tyne and Wear, all the top ten private manufacturing firms have reduced employment in response to a variety of 'restructuring' or 'rationalization' programmes (Figure 2.2). Northern Engineering Industries (NEI), a group formed in 1977 which incorporates some of the major Tyneside engineering firms (Clarke Chapman, Reyrolle, Parsons), has witnessed a long series of redundancies, a decline of 7000 jobs over the last ten years and a shift towards overseas investment. Plessey has shut down its telecommunication plants in Sunderland and South Shields, concentrating on production elsewhere in the UK and overseas. Vickers has completely reorganized production, closing the old Elswick and Scotswood works and building a new factory making tanks at the Scotswood site within the Enterprise Zone: employment was down to just over 300 in 1985 (NE Trade Union Studies Information Unit, 1985).

Shipbuilding, coal-mining, and steel have experienced severe cut-backs in the last few years. Between 1979 and 1985 the shipyards on the Tyne and Wear lost about 10 000 jobs and privatization has not succeeded in staving off further cuts in capacity and jobs either in the merchant yards or in Swan Hunter's naval yards. In coal-mining, the closure programme has been accelerated since the end of the 1984/5 dispute, involving even further concentration on the remaining large coastal collieries. In steel, the closure of the Consett works produced 3 500 redundancies and left this isolated single-industry town in serious difficulties, comparable to the position of Jarrow in the 1930s (Robinson and Sadler, 1985). Reports of redundancies and closures have also come from many lighter industries and from the branch plants attracted to the study area in the past with the support of regional policy inducements. Since 1980, major redundancies have been announced by many of the nationally known companies operating in the area, such as Dunlop, Thorn EMI, Timex, Ever Ready, Cornings glass, Ransome, Hoffman and Pollard, RHM Bakeries and Flour Mills, Ronson, Coles Cranes, Caterpillar Tractors, and WD & HO Wills. In addition, many lesser known firms, including in particular some large employers in the clothing industry, together with numerous small firms, have reduced employment through redundancies and also through 'natural wastage'.

These losses have been concentrated in the manufacturing sector while services have been less severely affected. Public sector services, although affected by constraints on public expenditure, have become even more significant as a source of employment owing to the pace of manufacturing decline. The DHSS benefits complex at Longbenton, Newcastle, is by far the biggest single establishment in the area and employs 13 000 people. The six local authorities in Tyne and Wear employed a total of 68 000 people in 1985 (compared with 69 700 in 1979) in a wide range of services. The National Health Service is also one of the area's largest employers.

There have, of course, been some gains in economic activity and employment. Undoubtedly, the most celebrated example of inward investment to the area is Nissan. The new plant at Sunderland, which started car assembly in 1986, is expected ultimately to employ over 2500. It remains to be seen, however, how much subcontracting work this provides for firms in this area and what effects Nissan will have on trade unionism and on the British car industry (Garrahan, 1986). Another recent Japanese arrival is Komatsu, the manufacturer of earth-moving equipment, which is setting up at the former Caterpillar tractor plant. 300 jobs are to be created, but this compares with over 2000 at Caterpillar's in the mid-1970s. There have also been some positive developments in the existing heavy engineering industry, notably increasing engineering construction orders for the offshore oil industry. In addition, there has been some growth in smaller firms, including new branches and new indigenous businesses. These elements of growth and investment are the main components which we focus upon in our subsequent evaluation of the effects of economic development policy. It must, however, be emphasized that the overall picture is one dominated by job loss; redundancy figures are still well above pre-recession levels despite the scale of past losses and the limited national recovery. This situation is only infrequently punctuated by good news of job gains.

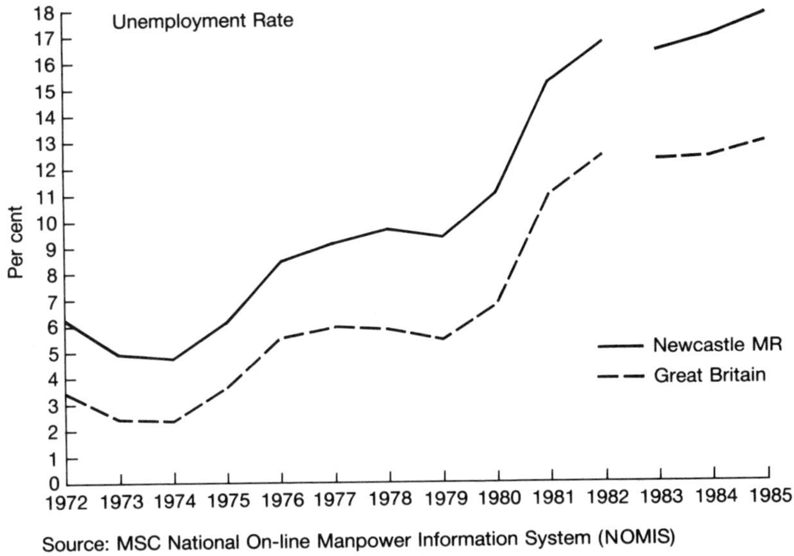

Fig. 2.3. Unemployment rates for the Newcastle metropolitan region and Great Britain, 1972–1985.

Source: MSC National On-line Manpower Information System (NOMIS).

Unemployment

Mounting job losses have led to continuing increases in unemployment (Figure 2.3). By June 1981, unemployment in the study area had reached 15.2 per cent. At March 1986, the area's unemployment rate was 18.9 per cent compared with 13.6 per cent for Great Britain and 19.0 per cent for the Northern Region. 94 005 males (22.3 per cent rate) and 35 116 females (13.5 per cent) were registered as unemployed *claimants* in the study area. 45 per cent of the unemployed have been out of work for more than a year and 36 per cent are under the age of 25. It is worth pointing out that these official figures understate the level of unemployment since they exclude people ineligible for benefit, those on MSC schemes, and those 'discouraged workers' who would enter the labour market if jobs were available.

There are considerable spatial variations in unemployment rates within the metropolitan region. Figure 2.4 shows the spatial incidence of unemployment in March 1986 at ward level amalgamated into zones (with the denominator based on the 1981 Census count of the economically active population). This indicates high rates in the older urban areas of Tyneside and Wearside designated as inner areas under the Inner Urban Areas Act. This concentration of high unemployment stems from several interconnected factors which link deprivation and vulnerability in the labour market to the

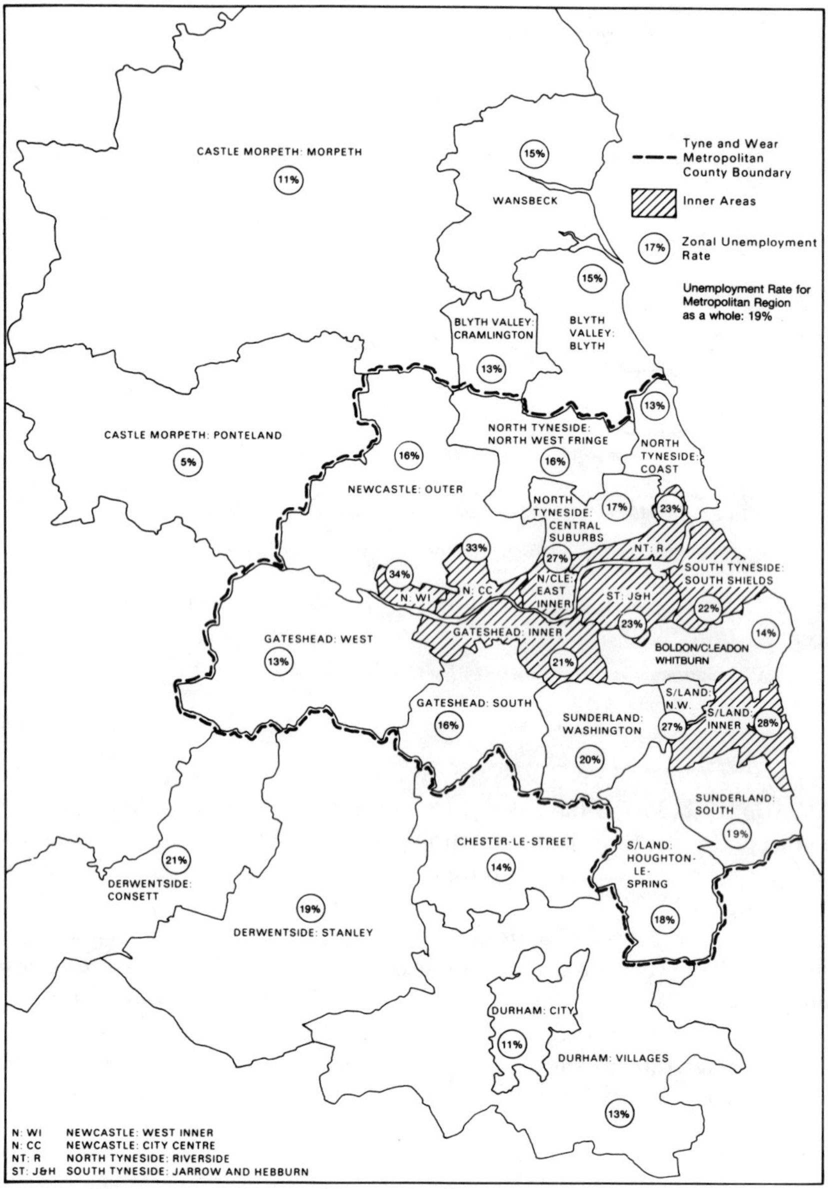

Fig. 2.4. Spatial variations in unemployment rates in the Newcastle metropolitan region, March 1986.

Notes: The zones were defined so as to identify the inner areas, retain the identity of major employment centres and relatively homogeneous residential areas, and respect local authority boundaries. The inner area defined in this Figure does not perfectly match the DoE designated inner area because some wards straddle the inner area boundary, but it is a close approximation.

Source: Department of Employment.

operation of housing markets; deprived residents in deprived areas are heavily dependent on job opportunities in declining industries within the areas of high job loss. All the designated inner areas recorded unemployment rates above the average for the area as a whole (19 per cent) in March 1986, but five non-designated areas were also above the overall average rate. Analysis of unemployment data for smaller areas—postcode sectors—in Tyne and Wear (Tyne and Wear County Council, 1985b) shows that the localities which experienced the most acute levels of unemployment (at July 1985) were mainly in the inner areas of the conurbation; the highest rate (46.8 per cent at July 1985) was recorded in Sunderland's East End, followed by Elswick Park in inner Newcastle, with a rate of 46.1 per cent. However, some peripheral estates also have very high rates, notably Newbiggin Hall estate in Newcastle (36.1 per cent at July 1985) and Thorney Close, Sunderland (33.0 per cent rate).

To what extent do these variations in unemployment rates reflect the pattern of job losses and gains? There is a considerable divergence between a very few areas which experienced employment growth between 1971 and 1981 and very many others affected by decline (Figure 2.5). The greatest percentage decline was in the Consett area following the steelworks closure. Several areas—notably Bedlington in Northumberland, East Boldon on the edge of Tyne and Wear, and also Sunderland—were affected by pit closures over this period, while inner areas within Tyneside and Wearside lost substantial proportions of jobs in engineering. Most of the older inner industrial and coalfield areas had rates of decline in excess of the average (−9.7 per cent) for the whole study area. Local factors, such as greater structural diversity and the growth of services, helped to reduce the rate of loss in some areas. In contrast, employment growth was confined to a few locations, notably the new towns of Washington, Cramlington (Northumberland) and Killingworth, and the County towns of Morpeth and Durham. The new towns, with greenfield sites and industrial estates, succeeded in attracting a large share of branch plant developments in the 1970s and thus gained considerably from regional policy measures and also, as growing centres of population, acquired service sector employment. They thus contributed to the suburbanization of population and economic activity. Durham and Morpeth, both growing in population, gained services and some manufacturing industry. However, the pattern of employment change across the study area is not *simply* one of inner urban area decline and suburban growth, not least because of the influence of the coalfield and of Consett; nevertheless, this is a dimension of the distribution and one which, in the case of the new towns, reflects the operation of public policy.

The high rates of unemployment (principally, but not exclusively, in the inner areas) therefore reflect both the pattern of job loss in the area and also the functioning of spatial labour markets. High *local* rates of unemployment must be seen in the context of an overall shortfall in the demand for labour

Fig. 2.5. Spatial variations in employment change in the Newcastle metropolitan region, 1971–1981.

Source: Annual Census of Employment. Department of Employment.

throughout the metropolitan region. It is clear that unemployment constitutes the most important economic, social, and political problem in the area.

The Structural Problems of the Metropolitan Economy

While recognizing that unemployment, economic decline, and de-industrialization are problems of the national economy as a whole, there are certain features of the Newcastle metropolitan region economy which are detrimental or problematic in relation to its development and which have contributed to its above-average level of unemployment. Some of these features may be amenable to policy intervention, others not; but consideration of these issues serves to indicate possible objectives for policy and the limitations of policy.

Research undertaken since the late 1970s has established a degree of consensus about the major characteristics and weaknesses of the economy of the Northern Region and these weaknesses also generally apply to the Newcastle area or have particular implications for its development (Goddard, 1983). Firstly, there has been a strong emphasis and dependence on heavy manufacturing and coal-mining—industries undergoing long-term decline and experiencing major difficulties competing with low-cost producers in world markets which are, generally, contracting. The manufacturing sector, now a relatively small part of the area's economy, has continued to be dominated by engineering and shipbuilding; these industries still provided 47.6 per cent of manufacturing jobs in the study area in 1981, compared with 50.6 per cent in 1961. Regional policy has resulted in some diversification (and this includes diversification *within* engineering), but not sufficient to fundamentally change the economic structure or make it significantly less vulnerable to recession. A related feature of the economy, stemming from the limited extent of diversification, is that there is an underrepresentation of 'growth industries'. Information technology, biotechnology, and robotics—those industries which may lead growth in the future—are not well represented in the area. There is not, for example, a nucleus of IT production in the Newcastle area like 'Silicon Glen' in Scotland.

Secondly, about 80 per cent of manufacturing employment is in establishments which have their headquarters outside the Newcastle metropolitan region and this external control has rendered many branch plants in the area susceptible to job losses in conditions of recession. The corporately marginal and geographically peripheral branches have often borne the brunt of contractions and closures during the recession (Townsend, 1983). Moreover, the vulnerability, short life-span, and lack of adaptability of many branch plants in the area have been heightened by their emphasis on routinized production of mature products, lack of R. & D. capacity to develop new or improved products, and an underrepresentation of higher-level management functions.

In addition, the 'branch plant economy' is poorly integrated into the local economy in terms of supply linkages and does not tend to provide a mechanism for the achievement of 'self-sustaining' growth (NRST, 1977, p. 52). Regional policy which, during earlier periods of growth and economic restructuring, promoted the transfer of branches to the area has helped to generate the development of this 'branch plant economy'.

Since the mid-1970s, however, the reduction in industrial mobility has meant that the take-over of 'indigenous' firms has been the main process contributing to the externalization of control. Such take-overs have often involved efforts to remove competition or take control of innovations; the result has been 'rationalization', including job losses (Smith, 1986). A third factor is that 'the small business sector of Northern England is less developed than in most other UK regions and shows little sign of catching up' (Storey, 1985, p. 9). The North has fewer small firms and a smaller percentage of people in self-employment than any other region (NECCA, 1986, p. 3). In Tyne and Wear, only just over 5 per cent of manufacturing jobs in 1981 were in local new businesses established since 1965 (Tyne and Wear County Council, 1986). Formation rates are relatively low in the North; in 1983 the region was in sixth place in terms of formation rates out of the eleven standard regions of the UK (Ganguly, 1984). Moreover, the failure rate of new businesses is high—more than 30 per cent cease trading within three years of start-up—and their contribution to the creation of new employment is modest. In addition, because of the industrial structure of existing businesses, the relatively low levels of wealth, and high proportion of blue-collar workers in the North, new businesses formed here are less likely to grow into large firms (Whittington, 1984).

Fourthly, the region has not participated significantly in the national expansion of private producer services. The growth of external control, particularly through acquisition of local companies, has resulted in the removal of headquarters staff and a decline in demand from industry for local services, these being increasingly provided from corporate headquarters. In particular, financial services are poorly developed in the area and this increases the difficulty for smaller companies in obtaining suitable packages of finance. In 1981, only 4.4 per cent of jobs in the Newcastle metropolitan region were in the growing sector of insurance, banking, and finance, compared with 6.2 per cent in Great Britain as a whole and 7.3 per cent in the Bristol region (Boddy *et al* 1986, p. 21). There is, in general, a significant underrepresentation of higher-order producer services, and professional and managerial employment (Green, 1985).

Finally, a high proportion of the area's employment is in the public sector—both the nationalized industries and public services. Decisions concerning investment and employment in this sector are taken by Government in the context of efforts to reduce public expenditure. Moreover, with the exception of regional industrial policy, the distribution of resources through the expenditure of Government departments is not explicitly planned so as to differentiate between regions; there is no explicit 'regional dimension' (NECCA, 1984). This is a crucial issue since the impacts are very substantial yet these aspects of economic development do not form part of spatial economic policy.

Briefly stated, these are some of the key *local* features of the metropolitan economy; initiatives to strengthen this economy and deal with the general problems of unemployment and the specific problems of the inner areas need to be seen in this context. Without prejudging the issue, it is fair to say that policy intervention has been, and remains, limited in its application to the types of problems we have identified.

3

Public Policy Responses to Economic Change

Rising unemployment in the Newcastle metropolitan region has promoted an extraordinary expansion of local economic development policy and a proliferation of agencies and initiatives, particularly since the onset of deepening recession in 1979. Regional policy has continued to be the most significant element of public policy devoted to economic development in the area, but there was a shift in emphasis and interest at central government level in the mid-1970s away from regional problems towards urban and inner city problems. The current Urban Programme, expanded by the Department of the Environment (D.o.E.) in 1978, provided resources for economic development policy in Tyne and Wear—and other conurbations—enabling the much greater involvement by the local authorities in economic policy (Howl, 1981; Burns, 1980; Buswell, 1983; RTPI, 1985). The more adverse economic climate resulted in a much reduced amount of mobile industry and hence attention also shifted to indigenous development and policies aimed at helping small firms—this, too, stimulated the involvement of local agencies, especially the local authorities. Policy experiments at local level were mirrored by initiatives by central government, including the Enterprise Zones and Urban Development Grants. There are now numerous policy measures and agencies—particularly in the small business field—and a complex overlay of spatial policies has been created.

This chapter discusses the main economic development policies operating in the Newcastle metropolitan region over the 1974–84 period, focusing particularly on agencies providing financial assistance to industry. This account briefly establishes the basic mechanisms of policy and provides figures for total expenditure to indicate both the level of resources devoted to economic development policy in the study area and the relative significance, in resource terms, of the agencies and policy measures.

Policies Operated by the Department of Trade and Industry (DTI)

Regional industrial policy and selective financial assistance

The basic structure of *regional policy* has not radically changed since the mid-1960s, although it has been subject to a number of revisions. The prime objective of regional policy continues to be the reduction of spatial disparities in employment opportunities, with a recent emphasis on new business formation. Thus, the 1983 White Paper referred to the contribution made by regional policy in easing the process of change in areas which have been dependent on declining industries and encouraging the establishment of new businesses in these areas (DTI 1983, para. 1). Although a phased reduction in the geographical coverage of regional policy was implemented in 1980 and 1982, this did leave all of the 'travel-to-work areas' in the Newcastle metropolitan region with Assisted Area status. Following the Government's most recent review of regional policy in 1984 the revised travel-to-work areas in the Newcastle metropolitan region and the Teesside conurbation are now the principal Assisted Areas in the Northern Region. Expenditure on regional policy assistance in the study area has fluctuated, but the overall trend since the mid-1970s has been downwards. From a peak of £72 million (at 1980 prices) in 1975/6, expenditure fell to around £25 million in 1979/80 and peaked again in 1981/2 at £44 million. Since then, expenditure has fallen steadily, down to an estimated £12 million in 1985/6 (Figure 3.1).

The legislative basis for regional policy during the study period was the 1972 Industry Act (subsequently consolidated in the 1982 Industrial Development Act) and policy in England is administered by the Department of Trade and Industry (DTI). Nearly all applications for assistance from firms in the study area are handled and determined by DTI officials within the region: the DTI North-East Regional Office at Newcastle deals with all but the largest selective financial assistance cases and also administers the Regional Development Grant Office at Billingham, in Cleveland. The main thrust of policy is financial assistance to firms and the most important instrument has been the *Regional Development Grant* (RDG), an automatic grant on nearly all new manufacturing investment.[1] RDG payments are based on a percentage of the eligible capital expenditure. Prior to 1980 it was available at a rate of 20 per cent in both Development and Intermediate Areas and, up until the 1984 revision, was awarded at a rate of 22 per cent in Special Development Areas and 15 per cent in Development Areas. During the study period 1974–84, before the recent policy revisions, RDG was not specifically linked to job creation or retention—because it was a simple investment subsidy, assisted projects did not necessarily have to lead to increased employment. RDG payments have represented by far the largest part of financial assistance to industry in the Newcastle metropolitan region, with estimated expenditure, at cost prices, of nearly £229 million between 1974 and 1984 out of a total for Great Britain of more than £4000 million.

The next largest source of DTI aid is *Regional Selective Assistance* (RSA), which is normally available in addition to RDG and which is used to support projects which create or safeguard jobs. Applicants must demonstrate that the assistance is actually necessary to enable the project to be implemented and they must also show that the project and the firm have good prospects of viability. In addition, the greater part of the project must be financed from private sector sources and the project must serve to 'strengthen the regional

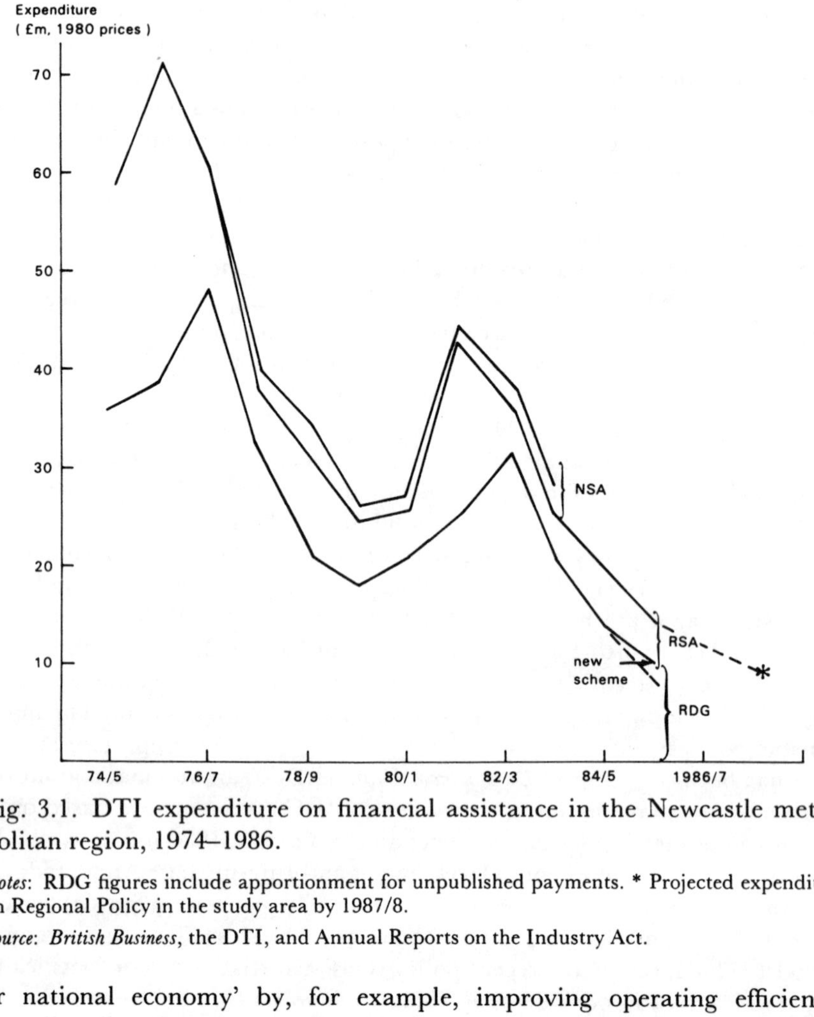

Fig. 3.1. DTI expenditure on financial assistance in the Newcastle metropolitan region, 1974–1986.

Notes: RDG figures include apportionment for unpublished payments. * Projected expenditure on Regional Policy in the study area by 1987/8.

Source: *British Business*, the DTI, and Annual Reports on the Industry Act.

or national economy' by, for example, improving operating efficiency. Broadly, all projects in manufacturing, construction, and mining may be eligible; assistance is also available to certain service sector projects (those having a genuine choice of location between Assisted and non-Assisted Areas). Our analysis reveals that over £86 million has been granted in Regional Selective Assistance to firms in the study area over the period 1974–84 of which only £8.4 million went to service sector establishments.

Changes to regional policy were introduced in November 1984, involving a planned reduction in total UK expenditure on regional assistance of around £300 million a year by 1987/8 (in 1983/4 regional assistance amounted to £690 million). Special Development Areas were abolished and a two-tier system introduced, with the core part of the metropolitan region granted Development Area status and the rest downgraded to become an Intermediate

Area. No changes were made to the eligibility criteria governing RSA, which continues to be available in both Development and Intermediate Areas. RDG, however, is now available only in some parts of the Newcastle metropolitan region—those areas which have Development Area status. RDG has also been made more directly related to job creation, it is less favourably structured towards large enterprises, and is now available to a few qualifying activities in the service sector.[2]

This study is largely concerned with evaluating policy over the period 1974–84 and therefore has not dealt with the effects of these changes. It is, in any case, too early to assess the impact of the 1984 policy revisions, not least because there is a major time-lag in the system.[3] Firms have been able to obtain RDG under the old system during a two-year transitional period (to the end of November 1986); and hence, as Figure 3.1 shows, most of the expenditure recorded in published data since the policy revision has, in fact, been made under the old RDG scheme. It is clear that RDG expenditure has continued to fall in real terms while RSA spending has changed little in recent years and is accounting for a growing share of regional policy assistance expenditure.

The DTI also operates *national schemes* under Section 8 of the Industry Act providing *National Selective Assistance* (NSA). This has been used to support firms in the 'national interest'—notably assistance for BL and Chrysler in the 1970s—and for general schemes to bring forward investment. In addition, it includes schemes of aid to encourage technological development ('Support for Innovation' measures); sectoral schemes for specific industries and small firms loan guarantees. NSA is available throughout the country with no regionally based eligibility criteria. It is of much less significance as a source of aid in the Newcastle metropolitan region than RDG or RSA. Between 1974 and 1984, assistance from these schemes to firms in the study area totalled £11.5 million, of which just over half was made under the Support for Innovation programme. The DTI has also provided financial aid to shipbuilding; figures for the study area are not available but committed expenditure on the largest element, the Intervention Fund, amounted to £251 million by 1983. On the basis of the area's share of shipbuilding employment and allowing for the structure of the industry, perhaps a quarter of this went to yards on the Tyne and the Wear.

Other DTI measures

In addition to regional assistance measures and national selective assistance, the DTI pursues a wide range of other economic development measures (for a detailed list of these measures see Walker and Allen, 1985). Many of these schemes are geared towards small firms and operate throughout the country—these include the Small Firms Centres offering general counselling and advice; various technical advisory services; and financial support for small firms offered under the Small Firms Loan Guarantee Scheme and Small Engineering Firms Investment Schemes.

Technological development is supported via National Selective Assistance schemes and also from the *British Technology Group* (BTG), backed by the DTI. The BTG was set up in 1981, combining the National Research Development Corporation and the National Enterprise Board. The BTG can provide finance for technical innovation through joint ventures, equity, and loan finance arrangements with firms. The function of the former National Enterprise Board, to provide venture capital specifically for developing new industries in the Assisted Areas, was abolished in 1984. The BTG did have an office in Newcastle and was very active in the study area before its functions were curtailed; it invested £5.6 million in firms in the Newcastle metropolitan region between 1976 and 1984 and this, according to the BTG, 'levered' six times that amount from private services. These investments are now gradually being relinquished.

Finally, the DTI supports English Estates which is responsible for factory construction in the Assisted Areas (see below) and the DTI is also the major sponsor of the *North of England Development Council* (NEDC). Established in 1962, the NEDC's primary role is to attract investment to the North from overseas companies. It works closely with the DTI, the local authorities (which also help to fund the NEDC), and the New Town Development Corporations and it concentrates on promotion and advertising.

Local Authority Economic Development Policies

Overview

All the *local authorities* in the area are now involved in economic development policy. In some cases this is minimal and includes little more than small-scale provision of factory units and industrial sites (Castle Morpeth District Council); in others it comprises a comprehensive Economic Development Policy and Programme (Newcastle City Council). The most active authorities—which have the larger resources and a clear legislative basis for policy— are the Metropolitan District Councils and the County Council in Tyne and Wear (up until its abolition in March 1986).

Comparable data on economic development expenditure by the local authorities are not available on a comprehensive basis since authorities differ in their interpretations of what constitutes economic development. However, the North of England County Councils Association has been assembling reasonably consistent information since 1979 on authorities' expenditure on the major components of economic development and this serves, at least, to indicate broad patterns and trends. These data point to a considerable contrast in the scale of economic development expenditure between the Tyne

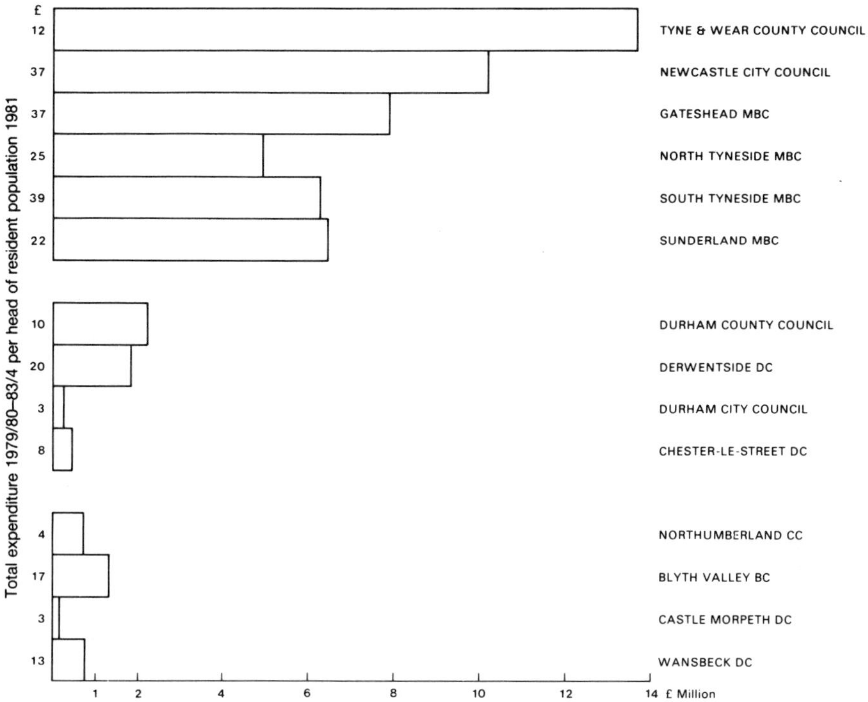

Fig. 3.2. Expenditure by local authorities in the Newcastle metropolitan region on economic development, 1979–1984.

Notes: Economic development expenditure here covers loans and grants; construction of factories; servicing and acquisition of land; promotion and publicity. Expenditure by Durham and Northumberland County Councils has been apportioned to the study area according to population. Returns were not made for the following: Derwentside DC (1981/2), Chester-le-Street (1979/80), Blyth Valley BC (1979/80, 1980/1, 1983/4), Castle Morpeth DC (1979/80), and Wansbeck DC (1979/80).

Source: North of England County Councils Association.

and Wear authorities and those in Northumberland and Durham (Figure 3.2). They also show that, in relation to population, even the expenditure of the most active authorities, the Tyne and Wear District Councils, is fairly small at £22 to £39 per head over five years. Between 1979 and 1984 local authorities in the area spent a total of £56 million on a whole range of economic development activities. Because of the way in which the NECCA data were compiled this is an underestimate, but, to place this figure in context, it does represent a level of expenditure amounting to less than half DTI spending on RDG (£129 million) over this period.

Since 1982 there has been a substantial increase in local authority economic development expenditure (Figure 3.3) as policy became more established and increasing attention was paid to economic policy concerns, and also as the emphasis in the Urban Programme, providing resources to the

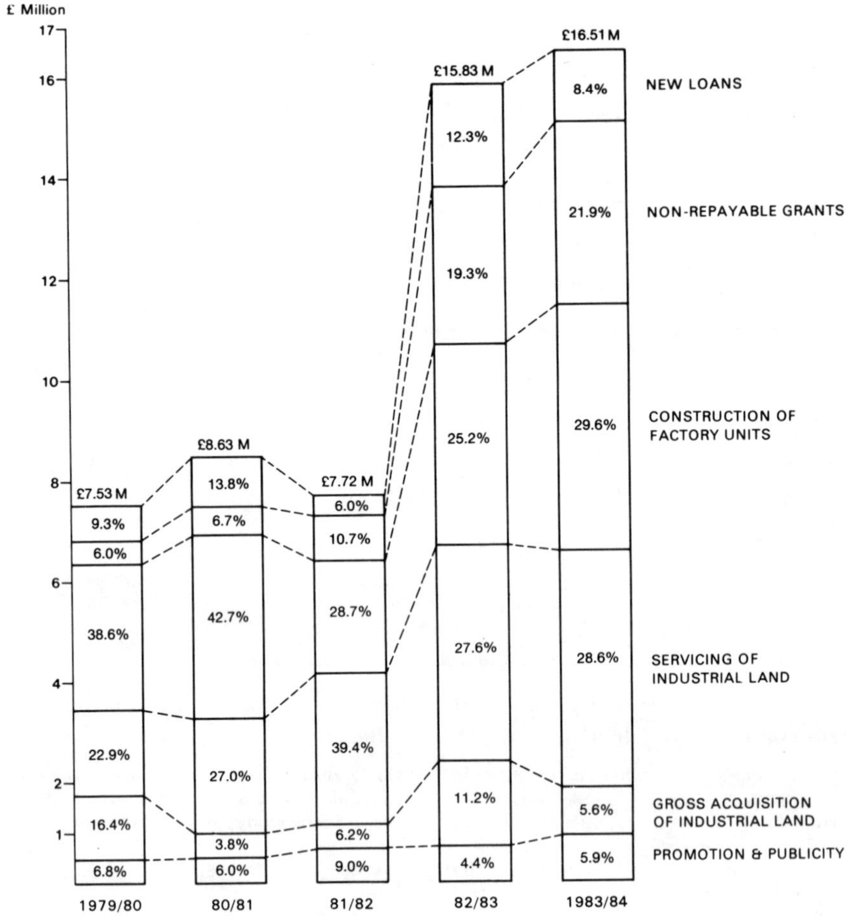

Fig. 3.3. Expenditure by local authorities in the Newcastle metropolitan region on economic development, by category, 1979–1984.

Note: Coverage of data as in Figure 3.2

Source: NECCA.

Tyne and Wear authorities, shifted more towards economic projects. There has been a considerable expansion of expenditure on grants to industry, but there has continued to be a strong emphasis on the 'traditional' areas of local economic development policy, particularly the acquisition of land and construction of factories.

Local authority policies in Tyne and Wear

Powers and funding Local authorities in *Tyne and Wear* first obtained significant powers to engage in economic development through the 1976 Tyne and

Wear Act, successfully promoted as a local Act of Parliament by the County Council. This provided powers to both the County and District authorities to offer loans and grants and declare Industrial Improvement Areas (Rogers and Smith, 1977). Subsequently, the 1978 Inner Urban Areas Act extended similar powers to designated local authorities in many parts of the country, and enabled these authorities to use the additional resources from the revised and extended D.o.E. Urban Programme (Lawless, 1981). The powers available under both Acts are very similar (see Figure 3.4). The main difference is that loans and interest relief grants for plant and machinery are available under the Tyne and Wear Act, but not under the Inner Areas Act—but this difference was removed in 1984 when Part III powers of the Tyne and Wear Act lapsed. It is worth pointing out, however, that the use of these two Acts in Tyne and Wear has been more closely related to the availability of finance and the procedures by which to obtain such finance, than with the powers themselves (Dabinett and Whisker, 1981).

The Metropolitan Districts of Newcastle and Gateshead were designated 'Partnership Authorities' and the other three Metropolitan Districts in Tyne and Wear were designated as 'Programme Authorities' under the Inner Urban Areas Act. Altogether, seven urban areas in England have Partnership arrangements while twenty-three authorities have Programme status. The Partnership Authorities have the highest priority for urban policy action, receiving an allocation of funds from the Urban Programme which is, nationally, four to five times greater than that for the next tier of areas, the Programme Authorities (D.o.E., 1986). The Partnerships also have a more elaborate administrative structure, involving closer and more direct liaison between the local authorities and central government (Lawless, 1981; PSMRU, 1985).

The Government's objectives for urban policy as a whole, stated in the '*Ministerial Guidelines*' (D.o.E., 1985a), are:

(*a*) to improve employment prospects in the inner cities, by increasing both job opportunities and the ability of those who live there to compete for them;
(*b*) to reduce the number of derelict sites and vacant buildings;
(*c*) to strengthen the social fabric of the inner city and encourage self-help;
(*d*) to reduce the number of people in acute housing stress.

Within the local authority areas designated under the Inner Urban Areas Act, Urban Programme resources are directed towards 'inner areas', which are those areas which have been identified as having the greatest social need. The inner areas of Tyne and Wear, defined by the local authorities in consultation with the D.o.E., are shown in Figure 3.5. Most of the powers of the Inner Urban Areas Act apply to the whole of the administrative areas of the Partnership and Programme Authorities but some powers apply only to the

Tyne & Wear Act, 1976	Inner Urban Areas Act, 1978
Loans (Part III) — Assist any person to purchase or take on lease of land to be used for an industrial building. — For the preparation or improvement of a site for a proposed or existing industrial building. — For the provision, extension, or improvement of an industrial building. — For the provision, extension, or improvement of services on which trade depends. — For any plant, machinery, or equipment to be installed in an industrial building.	*Loans* — Acquisition of land (S.2). — Work to land (S.2), site preparation works (S.9). — Installation of services (S.9). — Towards the establishment of a co-operative (S.3). — Towards the provision of access roads (S.9).
Grants (Part III) — Towards interest payments on local authority loans. — Towards interest on loans made other than by a local authority towards the cost of purchasing or leasing land, the cost of the provision, extension, or improvement of an industrial building, or towards the cost of plant and machinery. — Towards the rent of an industrial building or land to be used for an industrial building. — Towards the preparation or improvement of sites and services for use in connection with an industrial building. — Towards the cost of re-siting within the County of a business occupying an industrial building.	*Grants* — Towards the interest payable on any loan made to a small firm for the acquisition of land and the carrying out of works to land (S.11). — Towards the rent of industrial and commercial buildings (S.10). — Interest free periods are available on loans made under S.9 above (S.9). — Towards the establishment of a co-operative (S.3).
Industrial Improvement Areas (Part IV) Direct action by the local authority or assistance towards the following: — Construction of walls and fencing. — Exterior repair and painting. — Landscaping and tree planting. — Demolition of structures/buildings. — Construction of car parking spaces, access roads, loading bays. — Conversion, improvement, and modification of factory premises. — Improve amenities of area or buildings within it.	*Improvement Areas* (S.5 and S.6) The authority may offer loans and grants towards all the purposes outlined in Part IV of the Tyne & Wear Act and in addition: — Clearance or levelling of land. — Reclamation of land covered in water.

Fig. 3.4. Powers to assist industry under the Tyne and Wear Act, 1976 and Inner Urban Areas Act, 1978.

Notes: Relevant parts/sections of the Acts are indicated in parentheses. Powers under Sections 2, 3, 5, and 6 of the 1978 Act apply to the whole of the administrative areas of the Partnership and Programme authorities, while the provisions under Sections 9, 10 and 11 apply only to the Partnership 'Special Area'.

Sources: Tyne & Wear Act, 1976 and Inner Urban Areas Act, 1978.

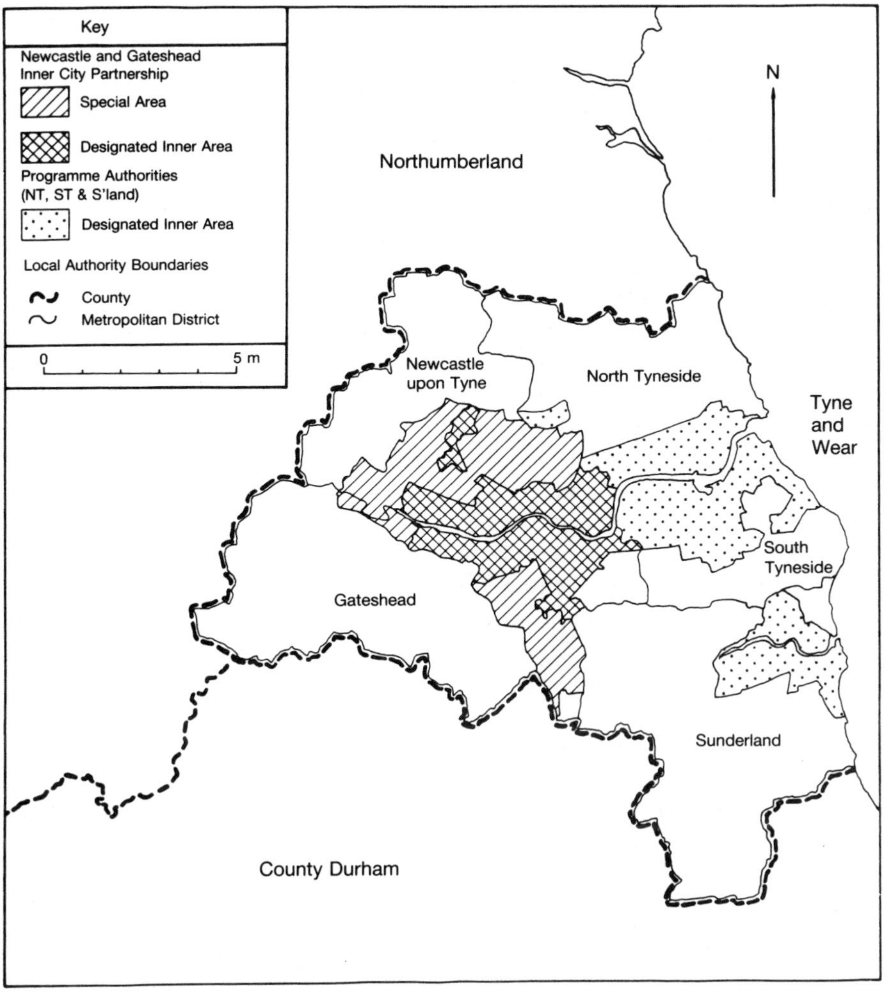

Fig. 3.5. Inner Urban Areas Act, 1978: Partnership Inner and Special Areas and Programme Inner Areas in Tyne & Wear.

Source: Partnership and Programme Authority Inner Area Programmes.

Partnership 'Special Area', an area which encompasses, but is more extensive, than the inner area. Notwithstanding this, Urban Programme resources are strongly concentrated on the designated inner areas and assistance from the Urban Programme is generally not allowed outside the inner area boundary.

For both the Partnership and the Programme Authorities an Inner Area Programme (IAP) is agreed with the D.o.E. each year comprising 'economic', 'environmental', and 'social' projects which will receive 75 per cent funding from the D.o.E., the local authority contribution largely provided from Main Programme budgets or through the 2p rate mechanism of Section 137 of the Local Government Act, 1972. Resources made available from the Urban Programme have, until recently, been growing but this has been offset by reductions in the level of Rate Support Grant. Between 1981 and 1985, the amount of Rate Support Grant to Partnership and Programme authorities fell by 16 per cent in real terms (Archbishop of Canterbury's Commission, 1985, pp. 177–81), significantly exceeding increases in Urban Programme allocations (Association of Metropolitan Authorities, 1986).

The Newcastle/Gateshead Partnership had a total IAP expenditure of £22.2 million in 1983/4 and the three Programme Authorities had a combined expenditure of £12.5 million. Within the Urban Programme an increasing proportion of expenditure has been directed to 'economic' projects and by 1983/4 more than 45 per cent of all IAP expenditure in Tyne and Wear was in this category (Figure 3.6). Total Urban Programme expenditure on economic projects in Tyne and Wear as a whole over the period 1979–84 amounted to £47 million, of which over half (£28 million) was spent by the Newcastle/Gateshead Partnership (Figure 3.7).

On the basis of an examination of local authority accounts it is estimated that about 45 per cent of the total economic development expenditure by the Tyne and Wear local authorities in 1983/4 formed a part of the Partnership and Programme IAPs. Of this IAP expenditure, 75 per cent is funded by the D.o.E. The Urban Programme therefore makes a substantial contribution to the economic development activities of the Tyne and Wear local authorities. The relative contribution of the Urban Programme does, however, differ between authorities. For example, in 1983/4, 47 per cent of budgeted expenditure in Newcastle City Council's Economic Development Policy and Programme formed a component part of the Partnership IAP, while only 35 per cent of Tyne and Wear County Council's economic development expenditure was within the Partnership or Programme IAPs. Examination of the local authority accounts also suggests that the relative contribution of the Urban Programme resources to the economic development activities of two of the Programme Authorities, North and South Tyneside Borough Councils, was significantly higher than for the Partnership Authorities, at about 60 per cent. The figure for Sunderland Borough Council (another Programme Authority) was much lower at 35 per cent, reflecting the larger resource base and higher economic development expenditure of this authority.

Finally, a further component of the Urban Programme, also dealt with by the local authorities, is the *Urban Development Grant* (UDG). This measure is intended to promote the economic and physical regeneration of inner urban areas by encouraging ('levering') private sector investment into these areas (D.o.E., 1983). UDG is available for capital investment projects which would not go ahead without some public sector assistance, but which, with that assistance, are commercially viable and help to deal with urban deprivation. Bids for UDG are submitted to the D.o.E. by local authorities, in con-

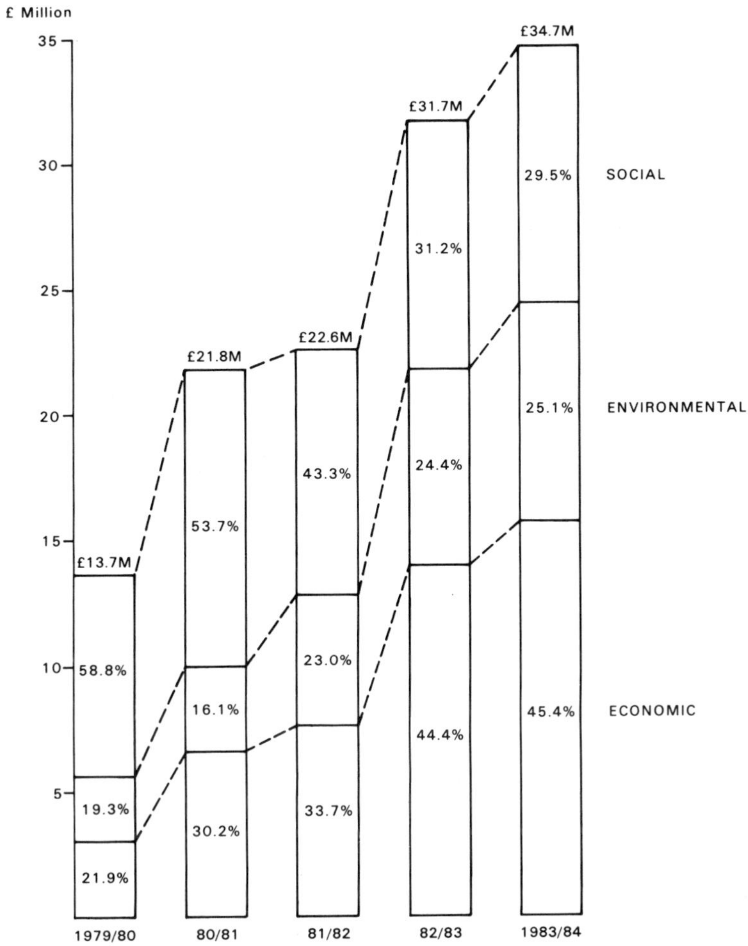

Fig. 3.6. Expenditure on Urban Programme projects in Tyne and Wear, by category, 1979–1984.

Note: The figures shown above refer to actual expenditure on projects in the Inner Area Programmes; 75% of the expenditure is met by the D.o.E., the rest by the local authorities. This covers spending by both County and District authorities. The percentage of total expenditure devoted to each category in each year is also shown.

Source: Inner Area Programmes and relevant local authorities.

junction with private developers. Proposals are then assessed by both the regional office and headquarters of D.o.E. If successful, the D.o.E. contributes 75 per cent of the UDG support offered, the remainder being funded by the local authority submitting the application. From its inception in 1983 up to June 1985, £5.8 million of UDG, levering nearly £50 million of private sector investment, was *offered*[4] to support 12 schemes in the designated inner

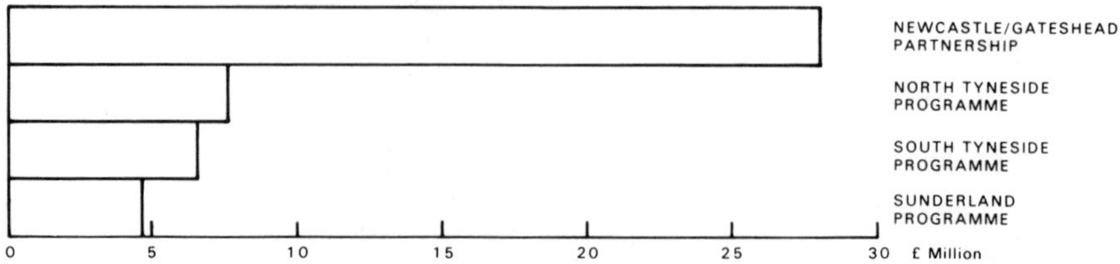

Fig. 3.7. Expenditure on economic projects in Tyne and Wear under the Urban Programme, 1979–1984.

Notes: The figures shown above refer to actual expenditures on economic projects forming part of the Inner Area Programmes approved by the D.o.E. 75% of the expenditure is met by the D.o.E., the remainder by the local authorities. The IAPs cover economic development spending by both County and District authorities. Because of definitional problems, the figures for expenditure given here are not directly comparable with he NECCA data on economic development expenditure shown in Figures 3.2 and 3.3.

Source: Inner Area Programmes and relevant local authorities.

areas of the Newcastle metropolitan region, involving commercial development (2 schemes) and housing (10 schemes). A further eight schemes had been offered UDG but had not yet started.

Policy Measures Local authority economic development policies are usually dominated by physical measures—land and buildings—and this is clearly the case in Tyne and Wear. All the authorities in Tyne and Wear are engaged in the acquisition and servicing of industrial sites and this has become a well-established function. Similarly, the construction of small industrial premises to rent has also become a legitimate local authority activity, catering for a perceived unmet demand. The third main common component of local authority policy is the provision of loans and grants to industry, a form of intervention which has grown significantly in recent years and is now also generally considered a legitimate area of local authority involvement. In a sense, these three broad categories of policy have formed the core elements of local authority action, leading on to the spatially co-ordinated approach of Industrial Improvement Areas where much of the effort and expenditure has been concentrated. By 1985, 23 Industrial Improvement Areas (IIAs) had been declared, under the provisions of the Tyne and Wear Act and/or the Inner Urban Areas Acts, and these are concentrated in the older urban areas along the banks of the rivers Tyne and Wear. Eleven Commercial Improvement Areas (CIAs) have also been declared in an effort to revitalize areas with shopping and other commercial activity. The aim of Improvement Areas is to improve operating conditions, restore business confidence, and secure employment through an interrelated programme of environmental and infrastructure schemes including the provision of new factory units (Williams, 1982).

There are substantial variations between the different local authorities in

Tyne and Wear in terms of their patterns of economic development expenditure and the specific types of initiatives they have pursued, even though the political outlook of the authorities is broadly similar (basically 'traditional' Labour) and their problems are essentially much the same. These differences seem to stem from a combination of factors: differing perceptions of problems and relative priorities; availability of finance; and organizational structures and arrangements.

Over the period 1979–84, the six authorities in Tyne and Wear spent £49.4 million on the five categories of economic development policy shown in Table 3.1. Of this, 39 per cent was spent on the *acquisition and servicing of industrial land* funded from various sources including the Urban Programme, Derelict Land Grant, and local authorities' main programmes. The County Council's role has been to provide two major strategic sites (at Boldon Colliery and at the northern approach to the Tyne Tunnel), suitable for new large-scale branch plants which might be attracted to the area; the County Council was also responsible for assembling land for the Nissan car plant which is being built on the site of the former Sunderland airport. The District Councils, on the other land, have generally concentrated on smaller-scale provision of industrial land. Site acquisition and servicing commonly forms an integral part of the programme of measures pursued in Industrial Improvement Areas, and of course, the provision of sites is often undertaken directly in conjunction with Councils' own factory construction schemes. Over half (55 per cent) of Gateshead's economic development effort has been devoted to the acquisition and servicing of industrial land, compared with only 25 per cent in the case of Newcastle City Council. This apparently reflects the narrower scope of Gateshead's activities, which have been dominated by the physical development priorities of the Planning Department, but also reflects the relative paucity of land which could be used for industrial sites within Newcastle City's boundaries.

The construction of factory units is the next largest category of expenditure, accounting for 31 per cent of total economic development spending in Tyne and Wear over the 1979–84 period. Almost all of this has involved building small units to rent, often at low cost and on short leases, for small and new businesses. In the last few years this has been increasingly linked to support services, with the development of managed workshops having on-site advisory services, secretarial assistance, and shared equipment (Martinos, 1985). There has also been an increase in the conversion of existing buildings for workshops, quite often drawing on financial support from the European Regional Development Fund. A recent large-scale example is the conversion of the former Plessey factory at South Shields to accommodate small business workshops and training facilities, a project undertaken by a newly formed local economic development organization backed by South Tyneside Council and the private sector. All the authorities in Tyne and Wear have built industrial units and all have now followed the lead of Newcastle City Council

Table 3.1. *Local Authority Economic Development Expenditure by Category of Policy, 1979–1984*

	Gross acquisition of industrial land (%)	Servicing of industrial land (%)	Construction of factory & units (%)	New loans & grants (%)	Promotion & publicity (%)	Total expenditure (£'000)
Tyne & Wear						
Tyne & Wear CC	12	28	29	20	11	13 700
Newcastle CC	9	16	24	42	9	10 200
Gateshead MBC	1	54	9	35	1	7 900
North Tyneside MBC	7	19	66	7	1	4 900
South Tyneside MBC	16	34	33	16	1	6 300
Sunderland MBC	6	30	45	15	4	6 400
(All Tyne & Wear)	(9)	(30)	(31)	(24)	(6)	(49 400)
Rest of NMR						
Durham CC & Districts	2	25	39	30	3	4 600
Northumberland CC & Districts	23	20	26	12	19	2 200
(Rest of NMR)	(9)	(23)	(35)	(25)	(8)	(6 800)
All local authorities in the Newcastle metropolitan region	9	29	32	24	6	56 200

Notes: Economic development expenditure here covers loans and grants; construction of factories, servicing and acquisition of land, and promotion and publicity. Returns were not made for a number of authorities and these are given in the notes to Figure 3.2. Expenditure by Durham and Northumberland County Councils has been apportioned to study area according to population.

Source: NECCA.

	TYNE & WEAR						CO. DURHAM				NORTHUMBERLAND			
	Tyne & Wear CC	Newcastle	Gateshead	North Tyneside	South Tyneside	Sunderland	Durham CC	Chester-le-Street	Derwentside	Durham City	Northumberland CC	Castle Morpeth	Blyth Valley	Wansbeck
Acquisition and servicing of industrial land	*	*	*	*	*	*	*		*		*	*	*	*
Industrial/commercial improvement areas	*	*	*	*	*	*								
Construction of factory units	*	*	*	*	*	*	*	*	*	*	*	*	*	*
Managed workshops	*	*	*	*	*	*								
Loans and Grants	*	*	*	*	*	*	*	*	*	*	*		*	*
Wage subsidies	*	*			*	*	*		*				*	*
Promotion and publicity (inward investment)	*	*	*				*							
Tourism promotion	*	*			*		*			*	*			
Advisory services	*	*				*	*	*	*		*		*	*
Technology initiatives	*	*		*		*								
Support for co-operatives	*	*		*	*	*				*	*			
Support for community enterprise	*	*				*								

Sources: Committee minutes and discussions with local authority officers.

Fig. 3.8. Economic development policies of local authorities in the Newcastle metropolitan region, as at 1985.

Sources: Committee minutes and discussions with local authority officers.

in building managed workshops (Figure 3.8). A recent new development in the provision of premises has been the construction of 'high tech.' units to meet a specific market demand.

Again, the share of expenditure given to factory construction shows significant variation between authorities. North Tyneside, for example, has regarded this as the most important type of policy intervention, with almost two-thirds (65.6 per cent) of economic development expenditure concentrated on the provision of small units—eventually, in 1984, the point was reached where supply was outstripping demand, vacancy rates were growing and building ceased. At the other end of the spectrum, Gateshead devoted only 9.2 per cent of expenditure to factory building; this is largely because of the high level of provision by English Estates in the Gateshead area, notably at Team Valley, and represents a reaction to problems of oversupply encountered by the Council in 1982.

Financial assistance, involving the provision of loans and grants to firms, accounted for nearly a quarter (24 per cent) of local authority economic development spending in Tyne and Wear as a whole (Table 3.1). Increasingly, this assistance has been provided in the form of grants rather than loans and is focused on small and new businesses. Early assistance schemes tended to be directly linked to local authority factory building programmes, providing rent relief to new tenants. More recently, schemes have been broader and more flexible. There is also now less of an emphasis on assisting manufacturing industry. Grants and loans have been given for a variety of purposes, including the purchase and construction of buildings, acquisition of plant and machinery, and, in Industrial Improvement Areas, assistance towards the cost of environmental improvements. Several local authorities have introduced wage subsidy schemes, supported from the European Social Fund. Some Councils provide grants for those starting businesses through the MSC's Enterprise Allowance Scheme, and a number of authorities have made special provision for assisting co-operatives.

Those local authorities with the highest proportions of expenditure on assistance—Newcastle, Gateshead, and Tyne and Wear County Council—were already offering assistance in the mid–1970s; others followed at the end of the 1970s. Newcastle City Council has been particularly active, generally linking assistance closely with other policy actions (aid to tenants of the Council's managed workshops, aid to co-ops, and assistance schemes to back up the work of local enterprise promotion groups). The County Council's role has tended to be more 'strategic', providing aid to medium-sized businesses, including new branch plants moving into the County. A large part of the assistance expenditure in Tyne and Wear has been funded from the local authorities' own resources (Main Programme and Section 137), but a significant part has been funded through the Urban Programme. Over the period 1981–4, it is estimated that approximately 35 per cent of total assistance expenditure formed a component part of the Urban Programme.

Apart from the three core activities—land, factory construction, and financial assistance—the local authorities in Tyne and Wear are involved in a considerable diversity of *other activities*, many of which are carried out by separate agencies receiving funding from Councils and often from other sources as well. An attempt is made to categorize these activities in Figure 3.8.

Several local authorities engage in the *promotion* of their areas in an effort to attract inward investment, and this includes advertising and participation at trade fairs. Most carry out some local promotion, involving the publication of business registers and the organization of local trade fairs to encourage local purchasing. Publicity campaigns, such as the recent 'Save Our Shipyards' Campaign which was funded by Councils in the area, are also a part of economic development activities. In addition, tourism promotion is a growing activity, in acknowledgement of the economic benefits to be derived from the tourist industry.

The emphasis placed on small businesses by the local authorities has stimulated the development of *advisory services* supported by local authority funding. In 1981, the County Council, with financial support from the Urban Programme and the European Social Fund, set up the Tyne and Wear Enterprise Trust ('ENTRUST') which now offers a range of services through its five local offices. These include advice for those considering self-employment; consultancy to assist business development; management training; and advice on community businesses (Eversley, 1985). ENTRUST also helps some local authorities vet applications for financial assistance. Other, similar initiatives, receiving funding from local authorities, include small-business courses at polytechnics and colleges, the appointment of community-based enterprise officers, and also the Business Opportunities Research Unit, an agency supported by Sunderland Council which helps with market assessments and information on suppliers.

A number of local agencies are concerned specifically with *technological development and transfer*. Tyne and Wear County Council helped to set up and finance the Tyne and Wear Innovation Centre, the Micro-electronics Applications Research Institute, the Newcastle Technology Centre, and a CAD-CAM (Computer aided design and manufacture) Centre. These agencies provide firms with advice on the application of technology in products and processes and can offer access to equipment. They are multi-funded—the Newcastle Technology Centre, for example, which seeks to establish links between research work in higher education institutes and industry, is jointly funded by Newcastle University, Tyne and Wear County Council, Newcastle City Council, and the European Community.

Finally, the Tyne and Wear local authorities have supported agencies encouraging the establishment and development of *workers' co-operatives* and, more recently, community businesses. The County Council and three of the District Councils have helped to finance the Northern Region Co-operative Development Agency, while Sunderland Council has supported the more locally based Sunderland Common Ownership Enterprise Resource Committee. Local authorities also often have specific grant and loan schemes for co-operatives.

To summarize, the local authorities in Tyne and Wear have generally been quite active especially in terms of policy innovation and development; some, such as Newcastle City and the County Council, have national reputations in the economic development field. On the other hand, it should be stressed that the majority of spending has continued to be on conventional areas of activity and experimentation has tended to be pursued through separate agencies supported by local authority funding. The Tyne and Wear authorities have not directly intervened in, nor sought to control, private businesses. In particular, they have not tried to emulate the examples of the GLC and West Midlands County Council which have set up an enterprise board to take direct equity stakes in firms, accompanied by participation in decision-making (Spencer *et al.*, 1986, pp. 145–8; GLC, 1985).[5]

Local authority policies in the non-metropolitan areas

Powers and funding The rest of the Newcastle metropolitan region outside Tyne and Wear County is administered by six District Councils, together with the County Councils of Northumberland and Durham. These authorities do not have the benefit of access to the resources, or powers, of the Inner Urban Areas Act or the Tyne and Wear Act (although Durham County Council does have some limited economic development powers provided under a local Act). Consequently, the opportunities available for pursuing economic development policy are far more limited. These local authorities are almost wholly reliant upon their own resources to undertake economic development and largely depend on the general powers available under Section 137 of the 1972 Local Government Act (as clarified and amended by the Local Government (Miscellaneous Provisions) Act, 1982). Section 137 allows local authorities to spend up to the product of a 2p rate on projects serving the interests of their areas, but not covered by statutory provision; this is taken to include economic development activities.

Expenditure by these non-metropolitan authorities in the study area is estimated at £6.8 million over the five years 1979–84. There are significant variations in the levels of expenditure between authorities (Figure 3.2). However, all have a much lower scale of economic development spending than authorities in Tyne and Wear—the £6.8 million spent by these authorities over five years was less than the expenditure of Gateshead alone. In Tyne and Wear, local authority economic development expenditure over this five-year period was £43.1 per head, compared with £16.2 per head in the rest of the study area. The Urban Programme accounted for a substantial part of the difference in expenditure, but even when this is excluded there remains a substantial difference. Overall economic development spending in Tyne and Wear, excluding the Urban Programme element, amounts to around £29 per head—still well above the £16 per head in the non-metropolitan areas.

Policy measures The relative lack of resources has meant that there has been little scope for experimentation, and the range of policies carried out by authorities in Northumberland and Durham has therefore been quite narrow and conventional. These authorities have very largely confined their activities to the three main components of policy—land, buildings, and financial assistance (Figure 3.8).

Six of the eight authorities are involved in the *acquisition or servicing of industrial land*. In the main, this is carried out as part of their own factory construction activities and the most active authorities are the County Councils. Durham County Council can purchase land for servicing or factory building under the 1963 Durham County Council Act, but did not use this power for acquiring land until it embarked on a factory construction programme in 1976.

All the non-metropolitan local authorities have built *small factory units*. In County Durham, this has often involved joint funding arrangements between the County and District Councils and also partnerships with English Estates and the Development Commission which operates in rural areas. In Northumberland, the County Council has built few factories since the late 1970s, but two of the District Councils, Wansbeck and Blyth Valley, have been quite active. In addition to the construction of nursery units, Wansbeck has recently provided rented office space with some common services while Blyth Valley has built managed workshops at a refurbished Council depot, part-funded by the European Regional Development Fund.

The Durham authorities—in particular, the County Council—have placed a relatively strong emphasis on the provision of *loans and grants* in comparison with authorities in Northumberland (Table 3.1). Durham County Council has, for many years, provided industrial mortgages under its local Act powers. Recently, however, the range of assistance has broadened and the bulk of expenditure is now in the form of grants, with assistance concentrated on the western and eastern parts of the County where unemployment is highest. Grants take several forms and can be offered in combination: they include rate and rent relief; interest relief; site preparation grant; small firms start-up grant; grants for consultancy; and a youth employment subsidy. The three District Councils in the Durham part of the study area have much more modest assistance schemes, providing loans and grants which are often in addition to those given by the County Council. In Northumberland, assistance has been a minor element of policy and has primarily involved small grants (less than £2000) to very small businesses (often with less than five employees). In the past, financial aid, provided by the County Council, was exclusively focused on the rural areas, but since 1982 this emphasis has weakened and the more urbanized Districts have developed their own schemes.

As Figure 3.8 shows, these authorities do little in other, more innovative, areas of economic development. Advisory services for firms are much more limited than in Tyne and Wear, and in some areas the Council's Industrial Development Officer is the main source of advice provided by the local authority. But new services are being developed; in 1984 the South-East Northumberland Enterprise Trust (SENET) was established, with local authority support, to give free advice and assistance to new and small businesses. In some areas there are, of course, other agencies fulfilling this role—notably in Derwentside, where the Industrial Development Agency provides an advisory service; this Agency has been primarily funded by the British Steel Corporation with some financial backing from the District Council as well.

Overall, these non-metropolitan authorities are certainly not at the forefront of policy development, not least because they have had neither resources nor powers. For some, economic development is still a new function and local authority organizational structures are still being adapted to cope with it. Most seem to have a quite strong commitment to economic development policy, but find it difficult to extend their current activities—they may look to the metropolitan authorities for ideas, but have major problems trying to emulate them.

Other Agencies and Policies

In addition to the DTI and the local authorities, a considerable variety of other agencies are active in the broad field of local economic development. These agencies and their activities are not easy to categorize on a systematic basis. There are many overlapping functions and interrelationships, and several agencies are funded from a number of different sources and pursue a range of initiatives.

Our intention here is to give a rounded and reasonably comprehensive picture of the various agencies and initiatives directly concerned with stimulating the development of the economy of the Newcastle metropolitan region. It is evidently difficult to define this area of policy since it may be considered that virtually all areas of public expenditure have implications for regional and local economic development. The inclusion of DTI regional and industrial policy and local authority economic development activities is clear enough, as is the inclusion of enterprise agencies and the public sector provision of factory premises. Beyond that, drawing a boundary becomes more arbitrary. The resulting picture is of a complex overlay of institutions and policies covering a fairly broad area of intervention in the local economy.

Provision of sites and factory premises

The public sector has played a key role in providing sites for industrial development and also building industrial premises. About three-quarters of land readily available for industrial development in Tyne and Wear is in public sector ownership. The private sector's involvement in factory construction is largely confined to extensions and purpose-built units; here the private sector builds few factories on a speculative basis and has participated in few partnership projects with the public sector (Chalkley and Perry, 1984). The principal reason for the private sector's lack of involvement is clear: the market here is difficult, characterized by relatively low demand, high risk, and low rentals.

The public sector agencies providing land and premises basically comprise the local authorities, English Estates, and Washington Development Corporation. The role of the local authorities has already been discussed. *English Estates* has been in existence for fifty years, having originated as part of the earliest regional policy efforts; it still has its headquarters at Team Valley in Gateshead, the first industrial ('Trading') estate developed by the then

North-East Trading Estates company. English Estates provides industrial sites and develops and manages industrial and commercial property throughout this area—and in other English Assisted Areas—on behalf of the DTI (and also, in rural areas, on behalf of the Development Commission). Traditionally, English Estates built large advance factories, mainly at green-field sites on the periphery of the conurbation. More recently, its efforts have been concentrated on smaller units (around 90 per cent of the newly built units are now smaller than 500 sq. m.) in response to the structure of demand which has favoured small units and made some large older premises virtually unlettable. There has also been more factory building in the inner areas and less emphasis on manufacturing—in a new departure, some office development has recently been undertaken. English Estates has also recently sought to broaden its range of industrial accommodation to include units specifically designed for 'high tech.' tenants. In collaboration with Durham University, it has developed the Mountjoy Research Centre at Durham for technology-based firms engaged in research and development and this provides links with the University's researchers and the Business School. English Estates offers financial assistance to tenants of their units in the form of rent-free periods, generally for a period of two years, and between 1974 and 1984 rent relief to firms in the study area amounted to £5.7 million.

Washington New Town was designated in 1964 and its *Development Corporation* has responsibility for stimulating economic growth through the provision of sites and factory premises, coupled with promotion and publicity, both in the UK and overseas (Holley, 1983). There are now around 12 500 jobs at Washington's industrial estates and the Development Corporation has built over 500 factory units. Up until 1985, the Corporation was able to build advance factories; since then, in the lead-up to dissolution in 1988, the Corporation's functions have been curtailed and it is now only able to build for specified tenants, but does have a stock of available units. Like English Estates, Washington Development Corporation usually offers two-year rent-free periods to new tenants and more than £2 million rent relief was given over the 1974–84 period.

Tyneside Enterprise Zone

Twenty-five Enterprise Zones have been designated throughout the UK since 1981 in order to 'see how far industrial and commercial activity can be encouraged by the removal of certain tax burdens, and by relaxing and speeding up the application of certain statutory or administrative controls' (D.o.E., 1981). The main incentives within the Zones are a rates holiday, for a period of ten years after designation, on existing and new property; 100 per cent capital allowances against Income Tax and Corporation Tax on industrial and commercial buildings; exemption from Development Land Tax (now abolished); and a simplified planning regime. The costs involved in the

Enterprise Zone experiment have been substantial and their benefits have proved difficult to quantify (National Audit Office, 1986).

The Tyneside Enterprise Zone, set up in August 1981, comprises old industrial land along the banks of the Tyne, together with the southern section of English Estate's Team Valley Industrial Estate. At over 1100 acres, it is the largest Zone in the UK and is also by far the biggest in employment terms, containing 12 500 jobs in 1984 (D.o.E., 1985b). There have been some significant new developments in the Zone since designation, notably Vickers' new tank factory at Scotswood and the £50 million 'Metro Centre', a huge (1.5 million sq. ft.) shopping and leisure complex under construction at Dunston (across the Tyne at Elswick, another complex, combining retail, industrial, and leisure facilities, to be known as the 'Armstrong Centre', is presently being planned). Small factory units have been built mainly at the Team Valley part of the Zone and this has included some private sector speculative development. In the period since designation up until March, 1984, the exemption from rates has amounted to nearly £7.3 million. The D.o.E. reimburses the local authorities for rate income foregone when they exempt firms from rates in the Enterprise Zone.

Total employment in the Tyneside Zone increased by 21 per cent over the 1981–4 period, but much of this seems to have resulted from short-distance moves within the conurbation and a distortion of development activity to take advantage of Enterprise Zone incentives (Roger Tym and Partners, 1984). Of the first round of the Enterprise Zone designations in Great Britain, the Tyneside Zone experienced the second lowest rate of employment growth between 1981 and 1984 (D.o.E. 1985b, p. 28). Considerable job increases will shortly result from the Metro Centre development, but it is also to be expected that this will, in turn, displace jobs elsewhere in the conurbation.

Much of the riverside land is derelict, with problems of contamination from former industrial activities, poor drainage, and access difficulties. The designation of the Enterprise Zone has undoubtedly helped to focus the reclamation effort on these areas in support of development schemes while a further initiative to restore the environment here is the choice of a site at Gateshead, next to the Enterprise Zone, for the 1990 National Garden Festival; work is now underway on landscaping this riverside site.

Enterprise and advisory agencies

The growth of economic development policy initiatives, largely centred on fostering small firm formation and growth, has involved the creation of many local agencies in the Newcastle metropolitan region delivering various kinds of advice and aid. Again, it is difficult to categorize these agencies and their functions. Most could be termed 'enterprise agencies' although here they have nearly all been established by the public sector with relatively little of the private sector involvement which characterizes the enterprise agency 'movement' elsewhere in the UK (Deloitte, Haskins, and Sells, 1984). This may be held to be due largely to two factors: the early involvement of the local authorities in small business development and, secondly, the relative paucity of large, locally based companies willing and able to sponsor such activities.

There are several long-established advisory services and agencies. The DTI operates the national Small Firms Service which offers information and counselling to help small businesses with their plans and problems. In rural areas, the Council for Small Industries in Rural Areas (CoSIRA) provides a similar service and plays a leading role in letting factory units built by the Development Commission. Another long-established source of advice in the study area is Enterprise North at Durham University Business School; established in 1973, Enterprise North gives help and advice through local panels of businessmen who act as counsellors on a voluntary basis. As discussed earlier, the local authorities support a number of advisory agencies including ENTRUST, SENET, and specialized agencies giving advice on technology, co-operatives, and community businesses. The local authorities also support 'start your own business' courses run by colleges in the area.

The private sector is relatively inactive in the economic development field. As elsewhere, there are employers' organizations, such as Chambers of Commerce and the Confederation of British Industry, and Small Business Clubs. The private sector has not, however, taken the lead in setting up enterprise agencies—although these agencies have succeeded in securing some support, in cash or kind (eg. staff secondments), from private firms.

A further, and increasingly important, component part of local economic development policy are the enterprise organizations established by nationalized industries in the wake of large-scale job losses. The first of these was *British Steel Corporation (Industry) Limited* which moved into Consett a few months before the steelworks closure in 1980 (Taylor, 1982; Robinson and Sadler, 1985). Subsequently, in 1982, BSC(I) handed over its operations at Consett to a local enterprise trust, the Derwentside Industrial Development Agency. The Agency offers advice, helps draw up business plans, and helps to negotiate assistance from other sources. Some aid has been directly available from BSC(I) itself in the form of loans and grants to firms: such assistance was paid to 130 applicants in Derwentside between 1979 and 1983, amounting to a total of £1.4 million. The BSC approach has since been emulated by the National Coal Board which set up a similar agency in 1984 called *NCB (Enterprise) Limited*; this operates in the study area and aims to help create new business opportunities and provide alternative jobs through the provision of financial assistance to firms, support for the retraining of miners, and helping existing local enterprise agencies (Sloman, 1986). Following recent (mid-1986) announcements of major shipyard closures, which are heavily concentrated in the North-East, *British Shipbuilders* is also establishing a job creation agency which will operate here.

The Manpower Services Commission

The Manpower Services Commission (MSC) develops and implements central government's policies in relation to the labour market. The MSC has experienced substantial growth, with total national expenditure rising from £685 million in 1979/80 to more than £2300 million in 1985/6 (MSC, 1986). This growth has been reflected in the Newcastle metropolitan region, where MSC expenditure is now greater than that devoted to either regional or urban policy.

Established in 1974, the MSC has responsibility for a range of training and employment functions. Its main objectives are: to safeguard the provision of skilled manpower to industry; to offer a range of employment facilities for employers and job-seekers, particularly those having difficulty in obtaining work or training; and provide planned work experience combining training and education for those under the age of 18 (MSC, 1984). These objectives have been pursued through a large number of schemes and programmes, which have frequently been revised and replaced. Since the early 1980s expenditure by the MSC on its employment services and occupational training has roughly remained constant, with the substantial increase in total expenditure due largely to increased spending on two major schemes: the Youth Training Scheme and the Community Programme.

The Youth Training Scheme (YTS) was launched in April 1983 to replace the Youth Opportunities Programme. The aim of the YTS is to offer young people (mainly school-leavers under the age of 18) a period of training and work experience. Originally, the scheme provided a period of work and training for one year with at least 13 weeks off-the-job training, but this has recently been increased to two years for 16-year-olds with off-the-job training lasting for at least 20 weeks. Participants on the scheme receive an allowance (£27.30 a week), and grants are paid to firms which provide places. In 1983/4, its first year of operation, expenditure on the scheme amounted to £770 million, of which about £30 million is estimated to have been spent within the Newcastle metropolitan region.

The YTS is now a major destination for school-leavers in the area. In 1983/4, for example, only 20 per cent of 16-year-old school-leavers in Tyne and Wear found permanent jobs whilst 40 per cent were found places on the YTS, 30 per cent went into Further Education, and 10 per cent became unemployed (Tyne and Wear County Council, 1985a). Currently (1986), only around 40 per cent of those leaving YTS projects in the Newcastle metropolitan region go directly into permanent jobs. The MSC is attempting, however, to increase this figure, notably through the recently introduced

New Workers Scheme, which provides a form of wage subsidy to encourage firms to take on people that have completed the YTS.

The MSC's main scheme for the long-term unemployed (in receipt of benefits) is the Community Programme (CP) which provides up to a year's work on projects deemed to be of benefit to the community. About two-thirds of the places on these projects are for part-time work. Projects include clearing derelict land, building renovation, and community care schemes. The CP has been progressively expanded: in 1983/4 there were 112 000 filled places nationally, involving an expenditure of £400 million, but the CP is now set to grow to over 250 000 places by late 1986 at a cost of over £1 billion annually. Expenditure on the CP in the Newcastle metropolitan region in 1983/4 amounted to around £30 million, supporting over 8000 filled places; by May 1986 the number of filled places had grown to nearly 14 000, involving an annual expenditure in excess of £50 million.

In addition to training schemes and 'makework' projects, the MSC has become increasingly involved in the promotion of self-employment. Through the Enterprise Allowance Scheme, unemployed people claiming benefits who start up their own businesses can receive a £40 a week allowance for a year; this is intended to help overcome the problem of loss of benefits faced by the self-employed. Again, this scheme has undergone major expansion since it was introduced on a national basis in 1983, and the number of entrants is set to grow from 65 000 a year in 1985 to 100 000 by 1987. Expenditure on the Enterprise Allowance Scheme in the Newcastle metropolitan region is now around £5 million a year (but this is the gross cost, not taking into account savings on benefit payments) and about 2500 people entered the scheme in 1985/6. In the last three years it has become an important way into self-employment in the area and, as noted above, some of the local authorities now provide financial assistance to people seeking to join the scheme who need to show that they have £1000 available to invest in their business.

The MSC has become a major agency involved in supporting local economic development efforts through labour market policies. Comparable figures showing expenditure on the various schemes are given in Table 3.2 which illustrates, in a relative context, the considerable resources now devoted to labour market policies.

The role of the European Community

The European Community plays an important part in funding economic development projects and initiatives in the Newcastle metropolitan region. Much of this finance does, however, serve to reimburse the UK Government for its expenditure on various programmes such as infrastructure investment and training. Nevertheless, some European Community finance is not tied to central government measures and is available for local initiatives: local authorities have increasingly turned to the Community for support, especially for those projects which are more innovative and unlikely to be funded by the Government.

Between 1975 and 1984, an estimated £60 million has been allocated to the area from the *European Regional Development Fund*, four-fifths of which has helped to finance infrastructure projects, such as the Tyne and Wear Metro rapid transit system. The rest has been allocated to industrial projects, but it is not additional—it serves as a refund to Government for DTI regional assistance spending. Tyne and Wear has also been eligible, as an area affected by the decline of shipbuilding, for funding from the former ERDF 'non-quota' section, which provided help for small and medium-sized enterprises through the provision of premises, infrastructure, and support for advisory agencies. The Fund was revamped at the beginning of 1985, a flexible quota system was introduced, and the 'non-quota' section was abandoned. A large part of the Fund is still devoted to infrastructure projects while the rest is to be earmarked for specific 'programmes' (*British Business*, 1986). There is a strong emphasis on help for small businesses, with funding to support the provision of converted premises and also grants from the new 'Business Improvement Services' scheme which was introduced in November 1984. This scheme, set up with the DTI, offers grants to small firms towards consultancy studies, market research, feasibility studies for product and process development, and also investment grants.

The bulk of *European Social Fund* expenditure in the area is provided as reimbursement to Government for spending on the activities of the Manpower Services Commission, but the Fund also supports some specific local initiatives, notably the Tyne and Wear Enterprise Trust (ENTRUST), the Innovation Centre, and wage subsidy schemes. The ESF provides 30 per cent to 50 per cent of the finance for wage subsidy schemes (now operated by eight local authorities in the area) which provide employers with a subsidy if recruiting the young or the longer-term unemployed. ESF expenditure on these schemes since they were introduced in 1981 amounted to almost £1 million by March 1984. Total ESF expenditure in the study area over the 1975 to 1984 period was estimated at £48 million.

A third source of funding comes from the *European Coal and Steel Community* which offers 'readaptation grants' to help fund early retirement, retraining, and income support measures in areas suffering job losses in coal and steel. This fund also provides low-interest loans to companies expanding in these areas. The whole of the study area is eligible for ECSC aid and, between 1977 and 1984, it received an estimated £30 million from this source. Loans are also available, at advantageous rates, from the *European Investment Bank* for productive or infrastructure investment projects contributing to regional development.

Overview: Economic Development Policy in Context

Our description of economic development policy in the Newcastle metropolitan region serves to demonstrate, above all, that there is a multiplicity of initiatives and policy measures in operation and a considerable number of agencies. This proliferation of policy is the most striking feature of economic development activities in the area and it does, undoubtedly, lead to some confusion and duplication. Indeed, many of the agencies have found that one of their main functions must be to help small businesses cope with this system, 'signposting' them to the most appropriate agencies and assembling packages of assistance from a number of sources.

A general picture of the main elements of economic development policy as a whole is given in Table 3.2 which shows expenditure (at cost prices) over the 1978–84 period of the key institutions or agencies active in the Newcastle metropolitan region. There are some problems with this data but none the less it does at least provide a reasonably reliable indication of the relative magnitudes of expenditure.

Expenditure by the DTI clearly represents a major component part of the overall pattern of economic development policy, accounting for more than £200 million paid in direct financial assistance to firms in the area over the period 1978–84. Local authority spending—which covers site acquisition and servicing, factory building, financial assistance, and other measures—amounted to an estimated £61 million, or considerably less than half the DTI expenditure on financial assistance schemes. Both English Estates and Washington Development Corporation comprise significant elements of the picture primarily because of their substantial investment in factory construction. Interestingly, the Table highlights the relative importance of Enterprise Zone rate relief which, at £7 million in the three years 1981–4 may be compared with the £13 million local authority financial assistance given to firms across the whole study area over the 1978–84 period. It also serves to demonstrate the very modest input of resources (£3 million) provided by the British Technology Group's investments in the more technologically advanced companies.

The lower part of Table 3.2 shows European Community expenditure and also, largely for purposes of comparison, the expenditure of the MSC. Much of the European expenditure also appears elsewhere under other heads because it represents reimbursement of spending by others, notably by the DTI and MSC. Much of it, such as expenditure on infrastructure and training, can only broadly be categorized as economic development spending—it may facilitate, rather than generate, economic activity. Nevertheless, with an estimated £125 million expenditure, the Community is obviously a very important contributor to public policy measures in support of economic development. The same is true of the MSC, which has spent over £150 million on training and work experience measures in the area between 1978 and

Table 3.2. *Main Areas of Expenditure[a] Relating to Economic Development in the Newcastle Metropolitan Region, 1978–1984* (£m)

Department of Trade and Industry			204
of which:			
RDG		146	
RSA		49	
NSA[b]		9	
Local Authorities[c]			61
of which:			
Loans and Grants		13	
Factory Building		20	
Servicing of Land		18	
Acquisition of Land		6	
Promotion and Publicity		4	
Other Agencies/Schemes[d]			65
of which:			
Urban Development Grant		6	
Enterprise Zone (rate relief)		7	
English Estates		32	
Factory construction & site development	(27)		
Rent relief	(5)		
Washington Devt. Corp.		16	
Factory construction	(11)		
Site development	(3)		
Rent relief	(2)		
British Technology Group		3	
British Steel (Ind.) Ltd.		1	
European Community			125
of which:			
Regional Development Fund		49	
Coal and Steel Community		28	
Social Fund		48	
Manpower Services Commission[e]			187
of which:			
Community Programme (from October 1982)		36	
Enterprise Allowance Scheme (from August 1983)		2	
Youth Training Scheme (from April 1983)		29	
Youth Opportunities Programme (1979–83)		68	
Training Opportunities Scheme (1979-85)		52	

[a] The expenditure by some of the agencies given in the Table has been used to fund the activities of other agencies. Thus, for example, the European Social Fund has been used to support the activities of the MSC and the European Regional Development Fund has contributed to the expenditure by the DTI.

[b] Excludes assistance given under the shipbuilding schemes; details were not available from the DTI.

[c] About 45% of Tyne & Wear local authority expenditure on economic development forms a part of the Urban Programme—75% of this expenditure is reimbursed by the D.o.E.

[d] Both Urban Development Grant and Enterprise Zone rate relief are administered by the local authorities. UDG is 75% funded by the D.o.E. (and is subject to D.o.E. approval) and central government reimburses rate relief to the local authorities.

[e] Details of placements on MSC schemes in the study area were supplied by the MSC. To obtain figures for expenditure, some allowance was made for the non-completion of courses and these figures were then multiplied by average national expenditures on each scheme.

Source: Relevant agencies and the North of England County Council Association (local authorities).

1984 and a further £36 million on short-term job creation schemes such as the Community Programme. MSC expenditure has been growing considerably in recent years while DTI spending has been falling, reflecting a shift in the emphasis of policy and expenditure away from direct industrial support and towards measures focused on labour supply.

Overall, economic development policy has been fairly conventional—concentrating on land, buildings, and financial assistance—which are considerably more important in terms of expenditure than the more innovative departures such as technology centres. It is also worth noting that policy has remained limited as a means of significantly intervening in the local economy. On the one hand, DTI policies which have been especially concerned with large businesses have been mainly pursued on a reactive, arm's length basis. On the other hand, the more pro-active policies pursued by local authorities and others have, by virtue of resource constraints, been aimed at the small firms sector. The larger firms, which have such a great influence on the local economy have—here, as elsewhere—essentially been subject to little policy intervention. They are, perhaps realistically, regarded as being uninfluenced by, or even beyond the reach of, economic development policy measures pursued at the regional or local level.

One issue of considerable interest is the changing balance between central and local government policy and expenditure. In terms of the actual *implementation* of economic development policy, central government's role may be seen to have been reduced—notably through the decline of expenditure on regional policy, a decline which reflects reduced commitment and doubts about effectiveness. On the other hand, central government has been devoting increasing resources to the Urban Programme, especially economic development measures, and there has been enormous expansion of the MSC. However, both of these rest on local implementation, with resources channelled through the local authorities and other public and private sector bodies. The Urban Programme, and also finance from the European Community, has helped to sustain and develop local authority economic development programmes in the face of reductions in Rate Support Grant. The local authorities (particularly in the Metropolitan Counties) appear to be at the forefront of policy development but much of their activity, in fact, depends heavily on central government funding.

The sheer scale of resources shown in Table 3.2 does appear impressive: by 1983/4 the DTI and the local authorities alone were spending £35 million a year on economic development measures. However, it can certainly be argued that this level of resource commitment is not large in relation to the size and severity of the problems involved. On the one hand, it may be compared with the Exchequer cost of unemployment in the area which is estimated to exceed £750 million a year (Sinfield and Fraser, 1985). On the other hand, costs which might be incurred in, for example, re-equipping a shipyard or subsidizing orders, might be expected to run into tens of millions of pounds. Even so, the amounts which have been spent on economic development policy in the Newcastle metropolitan region have been substantial. The question is, how effective has this expenditure been?

Measuring the impact of expenditure and determining the effectiveness of policy present many difficulties, ranging from the problems of obtaining basic data to problems involved in establishing and operationalizing assessment criteria (JURUE, 1981). In addition, as we have demonstrated, there is a multiplicity of agencies and policy measures, and this further complicates the process of evaluation. An assessment covering the whole range of local economic development policies is therefore not only difficult and complex; it is also likely to lead to somewhat limited and superficial evaluation. In this study we have, therefore, confined attention primarily to one particular type of economic development policy measure: the provision of financial assistance to industry. This has allowed detailed analysis covering different agencies and approaches. Financial assistance is a key component of policy and is perhaps the most amenable to evaluation. It represents by far the most important part of DTI regional and industrial policy and forms an important element in the economic development expenditures of local authorities and other agencies.

In the next chapter we begin our evaluation by looking at patterns of assistance expenditure. This provides the foundation for the subsequent examination of the impacts of assistance both on the operation of firms and on the labour market.

Notes to Chapter 3

1. Prior to the recent revisions in 1984, RDG was not available for small projects: individual items of plant and machinery costing less than £1000, or less than £500 in small establishments, and building costs below £5000. RDG has also not been available on second-hand capital equipment, and since the 1984 revisions it is no longer available on replacement investment.
2. The level of grant available under the new scheme of RDG is calculated as follows. For *small* undertakings (employing less than 200) and small projects the grant is now calculated at 15% on eligible capital expenditure or as £3000 for each new full-time job created, whichever is the *higher*. For *large* undertakings, only those projects creating jobs are eligible for RDG; the grant—for these eligible projects—is calculated at either 15% on expenditure or £10 000 for each new job created, whichever is the *lower*. For small undertakings carrying large projects (of more than £½m.) a grant ceiling is applied subject to the number of new jobs created.
3. The DTI itself has recognized this time-lag in the operation of policy; it does not intend to start a full review of the effectiveness of the revised scheme of regional assistance until 1989 (Public Accounts Committee, 1984).
4. These figures refer to offers of assistance; not all of these offers were subsequently taken up.

5. The five Northern County Councils, including Tyne and Wear, have subscribed a small part of their Superannuation Funds to the Northumbria Unit Trust. This was set up by Lazard Securities Limited in 1983 to promote a means whereby these authorities could invest in small regional companies, including unquoted companies. It is small, with £1.5m. invested in 1984 in 16 companies. Unlike the Enterprise Boards established by the West Midlands and the GLC, this does not involve control over the affairs of these companies.

4

Financial Assistance Policies: Patterns of Expenditure

Introduction

The collection and collation of data on financial assistance cases from the agencies represented a major part of the research. It is an important component of the study since this information, which covers the period 1974–84, serves to indicate the *sectoral and spatial distribution* of assistance; the relative significance of different *types of assistance*; the breakdown of assistance expenditure of the various agencies; and the extent of *multiple assistance*. This information has also been used to provide a sampling frame for our survey of firms.

The problems involved in assembling this information were initially underestimated and the exercise proved to be both difficult and time-consuming. Only one of the local authorities identifies, in public committee minutes, the names of firms receiving assistance; hence, access to data has had to be negotiated and assurances were required on confidentiality. Some authorities felt it was necessary to contact assisted firms themselves to seek permission to release data to us. Eventually, however, almost all the local authority data were obtained, although the local authorities were not able to separately identify those assistance cases which had been funded from their Urban Programme allocations. In the case of DTI assistance, only the published establishment-based data was available to the project: the DTI felt unable to allow access to data on the smaller, unpublished assistance cases, both because of confidentiality constraints and because considerable effort would have been needed to access this data from existing files. This is an unfortunate omission which has hindered the research. In addition to the local authorities and DTI, information was obtained from various other agencies, some of which supplied data without difficulty while in other cases detailed negotiation was necessary. Throughout this data collection exercise we were struck by the problems encountered in gaining access to data. These problems seemed to stem from two main factors: on the one hand, concern about confidentiality and, on the other, inadequate agency records which made it difficult to identify which establishments had received assistance and the amounts involved. In some cases it was necessary to provide help in searching through agencies' files to obtain these details. Some agencies were, however, highly efficient in providing data and readily understood the purpose and value of the research.

The information on assistance that we now have is much more comprehensive than that available elsewhere, despite the notable omission of DTI small assistance cases. Considerable time and effort was involved merely in collecting the data—let alone analysing it. To undertake evaluative work, such basic data are essential and problems of data availability appear to represent a significant obstacle to evaluation in this field.

Detailed assistance data were collected from the following agencies:

DTI—Regional Development Grant; Regional and National Selective Assistance. This largely excludes unpublished cases of assistance.

Local authorities—Data from individual County and District Councils, covering about 90 per cent of total expenditure.

English Estates—Full data on rent relief granted to tenants of English Estates factories.

British Technology Group—Full data on BTG equity investments.

Washington Development Corporation—Data on rent relief to factory tenants. This excludes those firms assisted between 1974 and 1978 which were no longer present in 1984; coverage is estimated to be in excess of 90 per cent of total expenditure.

British Steel Corporation (Industry) Ltd.—Grants and loans made by BSC(I). This covers the period to 1983, but very few awards of assistance were made subsequently.

In addition, *total* expenditure has been obtained for *Urban Development Grant* payments (channelled through the local authorities) and rate relief in the *Enterprise Zone*.

Scale of Assistance

The amounts of assistance provided by the various agencies and schemes are shown in Table 4.1. This covers a total expenditure of around £370 million over the ten-year period 1974–84. We have collected details of over 5000 cases of assistance—although the number of establishments receiving assistance is much less than this because many have received several awards of assistance from the same agency or from several different agencies.

The DTI dominates the picture, accounting for the majority of assistance expenditure. But other agencies, notably the local authorities, do have an important part to play—their resources are much smaller but are spread widely, often complementing rather than supplementing the activities of the DTI.

DTI assistance

The most obvious point to emerge from the Table is the *major importance of Regional Development Grant (RDG) and also Regional Selective Assistance (RSA)*. Of the total assistance of almost £370 million, RDG accounts for 62 per cent and Regional Selective Assistance represents a further 23 per cent. Altogether,

Table 4.1. *Scale of Financial Assistance by Agency/Scheme, 1974–1984*

Agency/scheme	Expenditure (£'000)				
	Amounts/cases known	Amounts/cases apportioned	Total	No. of cases	Average expenditure (£'000)
DTI	257 841	68 309	326 150	2 434[a]	108 4[a]
of which:					
Regional Development Grant	166 098	62 263	228 361	1 606[a]	103.4[a]
Regional Selective Assistance	86 255	46	86 301	483	178.7
National Selective Assistance[b]	5 488	6 000	11 488	345	33.3
Local Authorities[c]	14 596	280	14 876	1 909	7.8
of which:					
LAs in Tyne & Wear	13 444	0	13 444	1 605	8.4
LAs outside Tyne & Wear	1 152	280	1 432	304	4.7
Urban Devt. Grant [d]	6 374	0	6 374	381	16.7
English Estates	5 615	0	5 615	26	215.9
British Technology Group	2 416	0	2 416	249	9.7
Washington Devt. Corp[e]	1 446	0	1 446	130	11.1
British Steel (Ind.) Ltd.[f]	5 800	0	5 800	12	483.3
Enterprise Zone (rate relief)	7 253	0	7 253	NK	NK
ALL AGENCIES/SCHEMES	301 341	68 589	369 930	5 141	70.5[g]

[a] Total number of RDG cases unknown; the number of cases and average expenditure cited here refer to published cases only—it thus excludes RDG payments below £25 000.
[b] Excludes NSA assistance given under shipbuilding schemes and also the self-financing Small Firms Loan Guarantee Scheme because DTI data were not made available.
[c] Includes payments made to firms for Industrial and Commercial Improvement Area puroposes. Coverage not complete.
[d] UDG in this and subsequent Tables refers to offers of assistance made in the period from the scheme's inception (1983) to June 1985.
[e] Excludes some pre-1978 cases.
[f] Excludes assistance in 1983/4.
[g] Because number of Enterprise Zone cases is not known this average is based on total payments excluding those to firms in the Zone.

Source: *British Business* and relevant agencies.

DTI expenditure comprises 88 per cent of the total assistance expenditure from the sources identified in the Table.

As we have noted, the DTI information is not complete and the main problem arises in respect of RDG. Unpublished data on RDG assistance cases have *not* been made available, but the published information (which covers payments for amounts in excess of £25 000, which are listed in the DTI's journal *British Business*) records 1606 cases of assistance and an expenditure, at cost prices, of £166.1 million between 1974 and 1984. Expenditure on unpublished cases is estimated at £62.3 million in the study area (this estimate is based on apportioning expenditure, on an annual basis, in the same ratio of published to total expenditure as applies to the Northern Region as a whole). The *number* of these smaller RDG cases is, however, not known and cannot be estimated. On the basis of the estimated total of £228.4 million, nearly three-quarters of RDG expenditure in the study area has involved large payments—amounts of more than £25 000.

A substantial proportion of RDG expenditure has been devoted to subsidizing major investment projects and this is reflected in the size distribution of RDG payments. Of the estimated total RDG expenditure of £228 million, nearly half (£112 million) involved individual payments in excess of £100 000. Only 38 out of 1606 published RDG cases involved amounts of more than £500 000 but this 2 per cent of cases accounted for 13 per cent of published expenditure. The overall trend of expenditure on RDG has been one of decline over the last ten years, primarily reflecting the reduction in investment in recessionary conditions. In terms of constant 1980 prices, RDG expenditure in the Newcastle metropolitan region has fallen from an average of £32.7 million a year in 1976–9 to £21.8 million a year in 1979–82.

Regional Selective Assistance (RSA) under Section 7 of the 1972 Industry Act, provides grants and loans specifically to support the creation or retention of jobs. Published information covers 450 cases involving approvals of payments above £5000, which together amounted to an expenditure of nearly £86.3 million (there are, in addition, some small unpublished cases which have been estimated by apportionment). The figures relating to size of payments cannot be compared with RDG since these figures refer to total approved expenditure for specific projects, while for RDG each (large) payment in respect of a project is reported. Nevertheless, it is apparent that RSA, like RDG, involves some substantial payments in support of some major projects. The average approved expenditure is £178 700 per case, but 22 out of the full total of 483 cases have been for amounts in excess of £500 000 (Table 4.2). These 22 (5 per cent) of cases have accounted for 69 per cent of RSA expenditure—RSA has thus been heavily concentrated on a few projects at a small number of establishments.

National Selective Assistance (NSA), provided under Section 8 of the Industry Act, is on a much smaller scale and is more difficult to analyse since details of many of these awards of assistance are not published in the DTI's

Table 4.2. *DTI Assistance: Expenditure and Numbers of Cases in Selected Size Bands of Expenditure, 1974–1984*

Scheme	Expenditure size bands (£'000)								Total known expenditure and cases	
	0–25		25–100		100–500		>500			
	£m	No.	£m	No.	£m	No.	£m	No.	£m	No.
RDG	62	(NK)	54	(1 148)	83	(420)	29	(38)	228	(1 606)
RSA	3	(241)	7	(141)	17	(79)	59	(22)	86	(483)
NSA	1	(107)	2	(29)	2	(8)	1	(2)	6	(146)

Source: *British Business* and the DTI.

British Business. Again, cases of less than £5000 are not published, but a much more important omission is the non-publication of cases under the 'Support for Innovation' programme and related schemes (however, the DTI did provide some additional data on total expenditure and numbers of cases to supplement the published information). Total expenditure over the ten-year period is estimated at £11.5 million, of which about half (£5.5 million), comprising 91 cases, is published (Table 4.1). In recent years expenditure has been substantially lower than in the 1970s and this, coupled with an increase in the *number* of cases, has led to a decline in the *average* level of assistance. Average (published) payments were down to £20 500 in 1981–4 compared with £100 900 in 1978–81 (at cost prices). Only two cases over the whole period involved amounts of more than £500 000 and nearly three-quarters of cases were under £25 000. NSA approved expenditures have been, on average, much smaller than either RDG or RSA expenditures. Most NSA payments in recent years have supported relatively small projects under the provisions of sectorally specific schemes.

Local authority assistance

Local authority assistance involves a much smaller scale of expenditure than DTI assistance, but it has been spread quite widely. Over the period 1974–84, local authorities in the study area provided £14.9 million in financial assistance to firms; this includes assistance to industry in Improvement Areas and covers a total of 1909 cases. The average amount of local authority assistance was only £7800, and just over 66 per cent of assistance cases have involved amounts of less than £5000. Only 12 cases exceeded £100 000 (Table 4.3).

Local authority assistance expenditure has been growing in recent years, from a total of £3.9 million in 1978–81 to £8.3 million over the period 1981–4. At the same time, the *number* of cases has substantially increased, leading to a fall in the *average amount* of assistance, from £12 544 in 1978–81 to £5885 in

Table 4.3. *Local Authority Assistance: Expenditure and Numbers of Cases in Selected Size Bands of Expenditure and through Time, 1974–1984*

	Expenditure size bands (£'000)								Total known expenditure and cases	
	0–5		5–25		25–100		100–300			
	£m	No.	£m	No.	£m	No.	£m	No.	£m	No.
All local authorities	2.5	(1 199)	5.0	(493)	5.1	(106)	1.9	(12)	14.5	(1 810)
LAs in Tyne & Wear	2.2	(1 030)	4.8	(465)	4.8	(100)	1.6	(10)	13.4	(1 605)
LAs outside Tyne & Wear	0.3	(169)	0.2	(28)	0.3	(6)	0.3	(2)	1.1	(205)

	Through Time					
	1974–8		1978–1		1981–4	
	£m	No.	£m	No.	£m	No.
All local authorities	2.3	(80)	3.9	(312)	8.3	(1 418)
LAs in Tyne & Wear	1.9	(72)	3.6	(287)	7.9	(1 246)
LAs outside Tyne & Wear	0.4	(8)	0.3	(25)	0.4	(172)

Source: Relevant Local Authorities.

1981–4 at cost prices. This reflects, in particular, a shift in emphasis away from large loans and towards smaller grants.

There are significant differences in levels of expenditure between the local authorities over the period 1974–84. The six Tyne and Wear authorities, backed by legislation and able to draw on much greater resources than the non-metropolitan authorities, spent considerably more on economic development policy in general and assistance measures in particular. 90.4 per cent (£13.4 million out of £14.9 million) of local authority assistance expenditure in the study area was accounted for by the six Tyne and Wear authorities. The *average amount* of assistance was considerably higher in Tyne and Wear (£8376) than in the non-metropolitan areas (£4711).

Within Tyne and Wear, there have been considerable variations between the six authorities in terms of total and average expenditure on assistance (Table 4.4). In general, the *Partnership* authorities (Newcastle City and Gateshead Metropolitan Borough Council) and Tyne and Wear County Council (which is involved in both the Partnership and Programme areas) have spent significantly more than the three *Programme* authorities. This largely reflects differences in resources available under the Urban Programme. However, Sunderland Metropolitan Borough Council, a Programme authority, has a relatively large expenditure, most of which has been spent since 1981; this seems to derive from its relative size and, hence,

Table 4.4. *Scale of Financial Assistance by Local Authorities, 1974–1984*

Local authorities	Total	No. of cases	Average expenditure (£'000)
LAS IN TYNE & WEAR			
County			
Tyne & Wear	3 364	340	9.9
Districts			
Newcastle	2 971	374	7.9
Gateshead	3 470	256	13.6
North Tyneside	335	131	2.6
South Tyneside	906	127	7.1
Sunderland	2 398	377	6.4
(Subtotal)	(13 444)	(1 605)	(8.4)
LAS OUTSIDE TYNE & WEAR[a]			
Durham County Council (part)	1 139	118	9.7
Durham Districts (3)[b]	99	54	1.8
Northumberland County Council (part)	149	102	1.5
Northumberland Districts (3)	45	30	1.5
(Subtotal)	(1 432)	(304)	(4.7)
ALL LOCAL AUTHORITIES	14 876	1 909	7.8

[a] Only County Council expenditure by Durham and Northumberland within the study area is included, while UDG expenditure is not included.
[b] Excludes expenditure by Derwentside District Council.

Source: Local authorities.

resource base (Sunderland is the largest district in terms of population), and also the authority's commitment to assistance measures. Gateshead Metropolitan Borough Council accounts for the largest total expenditure—a sizeable part of it spent on Industrial Improvement Area assistance. North Tyneside Metropolitan Borough Council has the smallest total and lowest average assistance level—most of this expenditure was on small grants to quite small businesses.

In relation to those parts of the metropolitan region outside Tyne and Wear, Durham County Council has been, by far, the most active authority. The Durham Districts and the local authorities in Northumberland have spent little on financial assistance to industry.

Assistance from other agencies/schemes

The remaining six agencies/schemes shown in Table 4.1 altogether accounted for a total expenditure of just under £29 million, about 8 per cent of assistance expenditure over the period 1974–84. All the assistance from English Estates and nearly all of that from Washington Development Corporation comprised rent relief, while the Enterprise Zone assistance shown here is rate relief. The Enterprise Zone was designated in 1981, and, during the period 1981–84, Enterprise Zone rate relief (£7.3 million) was comparable in size to local authority financial aid in the whole of Tyne and Wear (£7.9 million). Urban Development Grant (UDG)is financed through the D.o.E.'s Urban Programme and represents a grant towards the cost of development projects (e.g. construction of industrial or commercial premises). UDG was introduced in 1983 and has involved substantial payments—averaging nearly £½ million—in support of some large-scale projects. Assistance from British Steel Corporation (Industry) Limited and the British Technology Group is also relatively recent. BSC(I) assistance was first provided in 1979, and involves loans and grants similar in average size to local authority assistance cases. Most of the British Technology Group's investment in local companies was made in the early 1980s. Between 1981 and 1984, BTG invested £3.1 million in firms in the Newcastle metropolitan region; its investment function was severely curtailed in 1984.

Form and Purpose of Assistance

Financial assistance may be given in various *forms*: grants directly paid to firms; interest relief grants; rent or rate relief grants; loans; loan guarantees; or equity. Assistance may also be categorized in terms of the *purpose* to which it is devoted: to subsidize the cost of buildings; other capital; land; labour; etc.

Form of assistance

The greatest proportion of assistance (87.3 per cent) has taken the form of grants (Figure 4.1). This includes direct grants (77.3 per cent of total known assistance expenditure), interest relief (5.1 per cent), and rent and rate relief (4.9 per cent). This is because of the dominance, in terms of expenditure, of DTI assistance, most of which has involved direct grant aid to subsidize investment. In addition, several other agencies/schemes have provided most, if not all, of their assistance in the form of grants (English Estates, Washington Development Corporation, UDG, and Enterprise Zone assistance).

With regards to loans, RSA was formerly a source of some large loans but this form of assistance has rarely been provided since 1979. Local authorities committed nearly half their assistance expenditure over the whole period 1974–84 in the form of loans and loans have continued to represent a significant element of local authority assistance, but the proportion devoted to loans has fallen substantially since the late 1970s. In recent years, local authorities have favoured giving many small grants rather than a few large loans and the majority of their assistance expenditure is now spent on grants (Figure 4.2). Loan guarantees have rarely been given, while only the British Technology Group has provided equity finance. One point that comes across

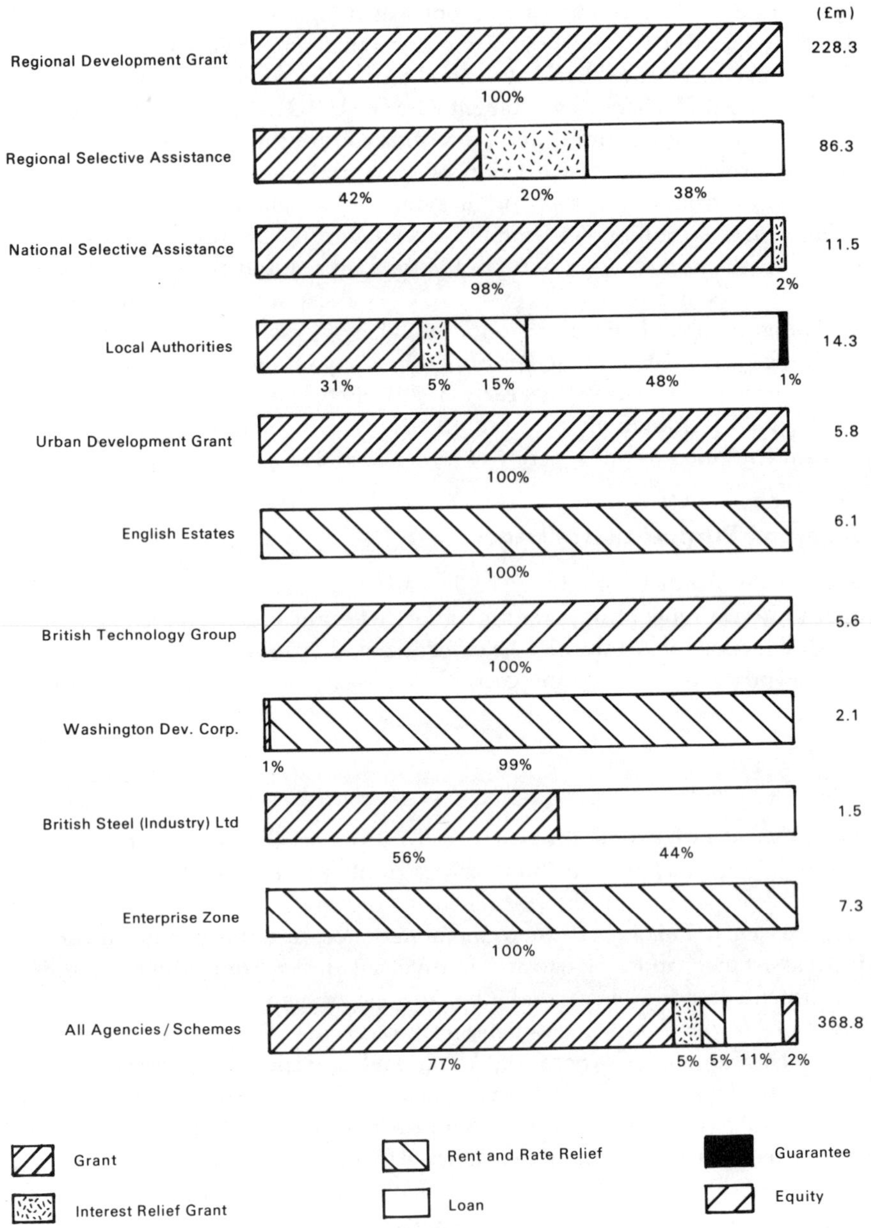

Fig. 4.1. Form of financial assistance expenditure, by agency/scheme, 1974–1984.

Source: Relevant agencies.

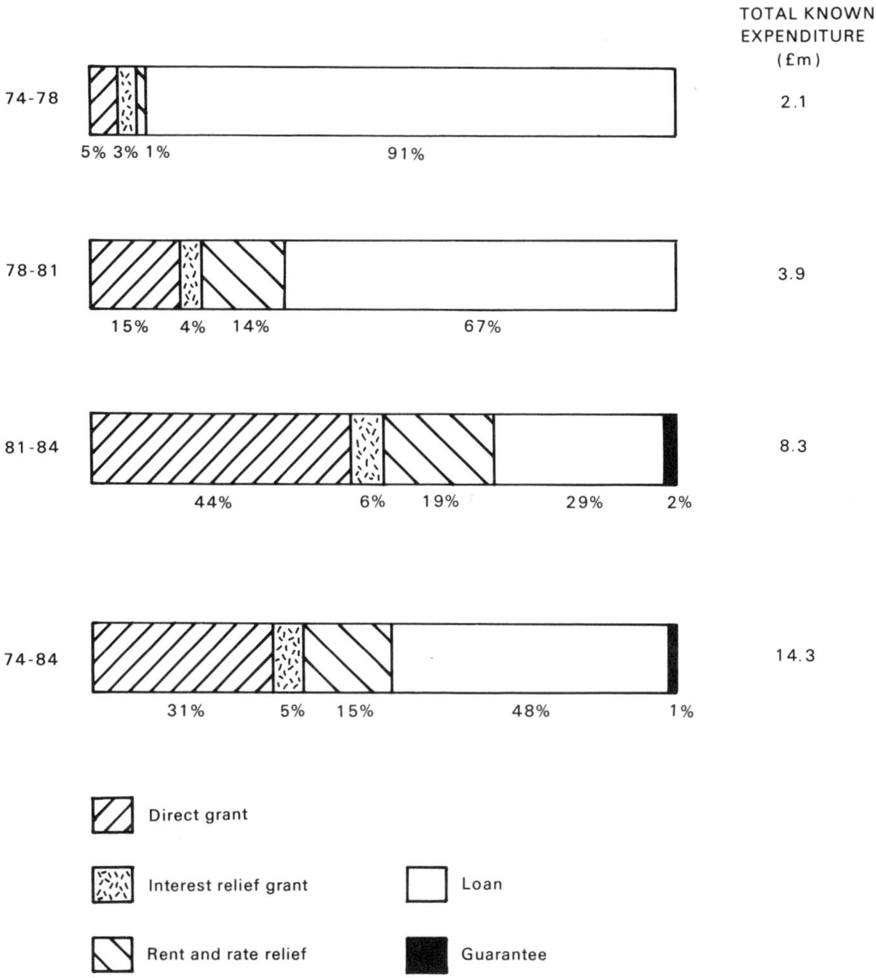

Fig. 4.2. Form of local authority financial assistance expenditure, over time, 1974–1984.

Source: Local authorities.

clearly is that the local authorities have operated through a range of forms of assistance, while most other agencies/schemes have been narrowly structured.

Purpose of assistance

A large proportion of the assistance expenditure which could be attributed by purpose has been used to support investment in plant, machinery, equipment, and buildings. All DTI assistance has been used to subsidize such capital investment, reflecting the structure and the underlying philosophy of regional and industrial policy.

Some of the other agencies, by contrast, have opted for the provision of grants, which, unlike DTI aid, are not tied to clearly defined and specified expenditures on investment. These include local authority start-up grants and rent and rate relief grants. Such assistance represents a general financial subsidy to assist the business and has the effect of increasing its cash flow.

Not only have the local authorities operated through a relatively broad range of *forms* of aid, they have also given assistance for a broader range of *purposes* than have the other agencies. The emphasis of local authority assistance has been on subsidizing investment, but nearly a third has been given as general subsidies, primarily start-up grants and rent relief (Figure 4.3). Local authorities have also provided assistance for land acquisition and servicing and, with help from the European Social Fund, have given labour subsidies. The structure of local authority assistance has changed since the late 1970s, marked by an increasing emphasis on (small) general subsidies and also by the advent of wage subsidy schemes.

Sectoral Distribution of Assistance

Analysis of assistance by industrial sector reveals that most expenditure has been concentrated on manufacturing. Of all expenditure which could be classified in terms of the activity of the recipient establishment, 88.0 per cent went to manufacturing establishments (Table 4.5). This is, again, a reflection of the focus of DTI policies which represent the bulk of assistance expenditure; however, it is also the case that all the other agencies have concentrated their expenditure on the manufacturing sector.

Eligibility for RDG has been restricted to firms in manufacturing and—up until 1977—firms engaged in mining, quarrying, and construction (although some payments have been made to companies which lease services, such as plant or equipment, to eligible industries). Major recipients of large RDG payments include establishments in mechanical and electrical engineering, with a total of £28.8 million; food, drink, and tobacco (£19.6 million); chemicals (£18.6 million); metal manufacture (£13.1 million); and shipbuilding (£13.0 million). Because it is a subsidy for investment, RDG has been particularly concentrated on these capital-intensive industries which have, consequently, received proportionately more aid than their share of manufacturing employment (Figure 4.4). It is, however, worth noting here that this describes the sectoral pattern of RDG expenditure prior to the revisions introduced in November 1984; these revisions had the effect of linking RDG more directly to job creation and hence there is now likely to be less concentration on capital-intensive industry. In addition, while the emphasis has remained overwhelmingly on manufacturing industry, the revisions did extend eligibility for RDG to some service sector activities.

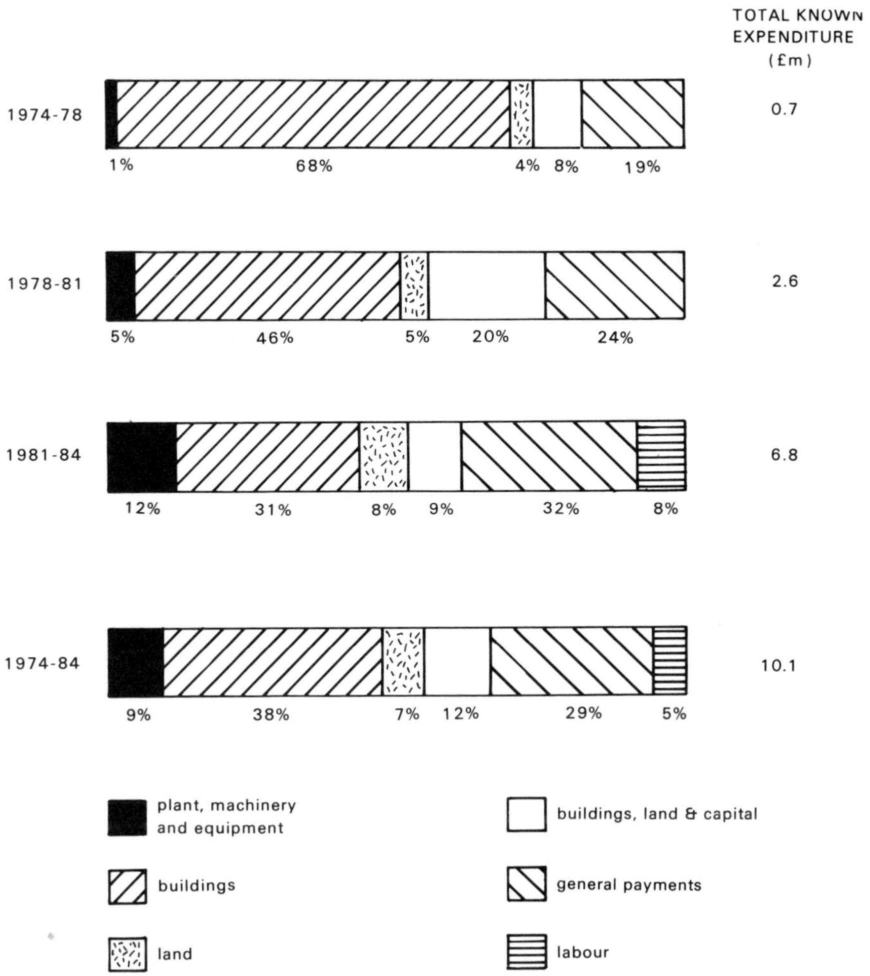

Fig. 4.3. Purpose of local authority financial assistance expenditure, over time, 1974–1984.

Source: Local authorities.

RSA has included some payments to service sector firms, principally to encourage relocation, but 87.6 per cent of RSA expenditure which could be categorized by industry has gone to firms in manufacturing, notably shipbuilding (£26.8 million) and mechanical engineering (£14.3 million). In the service sector, the distributive trades have been the main beneficiary (£5.6 million), but the whole of the service sector, with assistance totalling £8.4 million, has received less than mechanical engineering alone. NSA has been heavily concentrated on engineering industries, with over 86 per cent of

Table 4.5. *Sectoral Distribution of Financial Assistance by Agency/Scheme, 1974–1984*

Agency/Scheme	Sector (%)				Total known assistance (£'000)	Total assistance (£'000)
	Primary	Manu-facturing	Construction	Services		
DTI	3.1	88.8	4.1	4.0	216 757	326 150
of which:						
Regional Development Grant	4.9	89.2	5.9	0	137 182	228 361
Regional Selective Assistance	0	87.6	1.1	11.3	74 334	86 301
National Selective Assistance	0	95.3	0.1	4.6	5 241	11 488
Local authorities	0.1	72.9	4.1	22.9	12 881	14 876
of which:						
LAs in Tyne & Wear	0.1	72.6	4.3	23.0	11 881	13 444
LAs outside Tyne & Wear	0.3	77.2	1.3	21.2	1 000	1 432
Urban Devt. Grant	NK	NK	NK	NK	—	5 800
English Estates	0	86.3	7.8	5.9	4 271	6 374
British Technology Group	0	100.0	0	0	2 347	5 615
Washington Devt. Corp.	0	84.6	3.3	12.1	2 396	2 416
British Steel (Ind.) Ltd.	0.6	86.4	2.4	10.6	1 429	1 446
Enterprise Zone	NK	NK	NK	NK	—	7 253
ALL AGENCIES/SCHEMES	2.8	88.0	4.1	5.1	240 081	369 930

Note: The Table excludes RDG payments totalling £19.5m which were made to equipment leasing companies, as the ultimate beneficiaries of this aid are not known.

Source: *British Business* and relevant agencies.

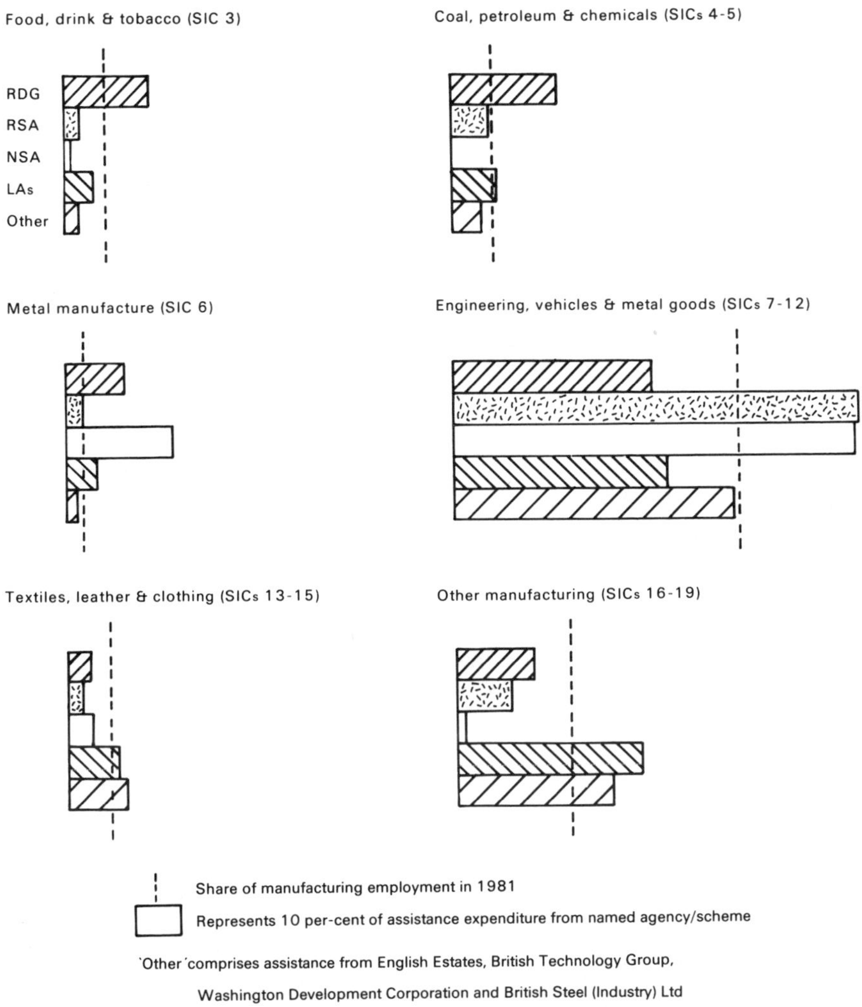

Fig. 4.4. Share of assistance expenditure within manufacturing industry, by agency/scheme, 1974–1984.

Source: Relevant agencies.

expenditure going to firms in engineering and also to foundries under the provisions of sectorally specific schemes.

Unlike DTI assistance, a significant proportion of local authority aid has been given to firms in the service sector—this reflects the number of small firms starting up and receiving small grants in this sector. Even so, nearly three-quarters of local authority aid has gone to manufacturing industry, with some emphasis on the smaller-scale, labour-intensive activities such as printing, timber and furniture, clothing, and 'other' manufacturing. It is, however, difficult to make direct comparisons with the pattern of DTI assistance owing to the problem of lack of data on the smaller, unpublished DTI payments.

The other four agencies for which information is given in Table 4.5 have an emphasis on aid to manufacturing. Tenants of English Estates and Washington Development Corporation, receiving rent relief assistance, are predominantly manufacturing firms renting factory premises. BTG's remit has stressed manufacturing and BSC(I) has mainly offered loans and grants to manufacturing industry. Enterprise Zone rate relief will also predominantly have assisted manufacturing firms owing to the nature of the areas covered by Zone designation (in particular, the southern section of English Estates' Team Valley).

The sectoral distribution of assistance is very different from the sectoral distribution of employment: only 5 per cent of assistance went to the service sector although this sector accounted for 62 per cent of employment in the study area in 1981. The implications of this, and its consequences for the impact of assistance policies, are discussed in Chapter 6.

Size of Assisted Establishments

An attempt has been made to examine the distribution of assistance in terms of the size profile of assisted establishments, with size defined as the number of employees. Such an analysis is difficult to undertake owing to deficiencies in data, but the results of the exercise are, nevertheless, revealing and useful.

As far as possible, assistance cases have been matched to a data base giving employment at an establishment level: a little over half the cases were successfully matched in this way. The data base does not include Northumberland, so the analysis covers only Tyne and Wear and those parts of County Durham within the study area. The data presented here refer to cases of assistance, so it should be noted that an establishment assisted more than once will be recorded in the figures for each award of assistance. The most important caveat in relation to the figures concerns, again, the absence of data for small DTI assistance cases; as a consequence of this, the size profile of DTI cases will be distorted towards the larger establishments.

Table 4.6 shows the size groups, average, and median employment of assisted establishments. Over half the *cases* of assistance identified in the Table went to establishments employing 1 to 25 people, but these cases involve many very small awards of assistance—hence only a relatively small proportion (12.6 per cent) of *expenditure* went to these small establishments.

Even allowing for deficiencies in the data, the contrast between agencies—especially between the DTI and the others—is substantial. The DTI has tended to assist mainly the larger establishments; the median employment size groups of the recipients of (larger) RDG payments was 201–500, while for RSA and NSA it was 51–100. The local authorities and other agencies,

Table 4.6. *Employment Size of Financially Assisted Establishments by Agency/ Scheme, 1974–1984*

Agency/Scheme	Employment size group (%)				Median employment
	0–5	6–25	26–200	>200	
DTI	2.7	9.0	24.2	64.1	348
of which:					
Regional Development Grant	2.1	5.1	18.8	74.0	484
Regional Selective Assistance	6.9	20.7	45.7	26.7	61
National Selective Assistance	1.9	33.9	32.1	32.1	54
Local authorities	36.4	42.6	19.0	2.0	8
of which:					
District Councils	42.8	41.8	14.2	1.2	7
County Councils	16.2	45.2	34.3	4.3	16
English Estates	19.1	49.1	25.8	6.0	13
British Technology Group	18.2	18.2	54.5	9.1	46
Washington Devt. Corp.	49.0	41.0	10.0	0	6
British Steel (Ind.) Ltd.	54.9	32.8	12.3	0	5
ALL AGENCIES/SCHEMES	23.7	29.0	21.2	26.1	21

Notes: An establishment which has received assistance under two or more separate approvals (or payments in the case of RDG) will occur more than once in this Table. The Table includes only establishments in Tyne and Wear and County Durham, as employment figures for establishments in Northumberland are generally not known. Employment details for firms receiving Urban Development Grant and Enterprise Zone assistance are also not known.

Sources: *British Business* and relevant agencies.

with much smaller resources, have concentrated their efforts on much smaller establishments—over half the BSC(I) assistance cases, for example, involved establishments of 1–5 employees.

The contrast between types of local authorities is of particular interest, revealing that the County Councils (especially Tyne and Wear) have tended to assist larger establishments than the District Councils: 84.6 per cent of District Council cases were in the size range 1–25, compared with 61.4 per cent of County Council cases.

The Concentration of Assistance

Here we consider the extent to which assistance from a particular agency/ scheme is concentrated on a few establishments or spread across many establishments. Is it the case, for example, that a small number of establishments receive a disproportionate share of assistance because they are in a particular industry or are engaged in a certain type or scale of investment?

The most useful approach to this issue is to determine the concentration of expenditure by calculating the *share* of total expenditure which has gone to

Table 4.7. *Concentration of Financial Assistance: Percentage of Expenditure going to the 10% Most Heavily Assisted Establishments, 1974–1984*

Agency/Scheme	%	Agency/Scheme	%
Regional Development Grant[a]	59	LAs in Tyne & Wear	46
Regional Selective Assistance	78	LAs outside Tyne & Wear	77
National Selective Assistance	61	(All LAs)	(49)
(All DTI[a])	(70)	Washington Dev. Corp.	39
English Estates	52	BSC(I) Ltd.	45
British Technology Group	26	(All agencies/schemes)	(84)

[a] Excludes small (less than £25 000) RDG payments.

Source: Relevant Agencies.

the largest recipients. The assisted establishments are first ranked in terms of the total amounts they have received from each specific agency/scheme. The largest 10 per cent of recipients are identified this way and the assistance received by this 10 per cent (the top decile) is then expressed as a percentage of the total expenditure (Table 4.7). This shows that all sources of assistance are characterized by a skewed distribution, with relatively large amounts paid to a small proportion of establishments. So far as DTI assistance is concerned, the highest degree of concentration was found for RSA: more than three-quarters (77.8 per cent) of RSA expenditure went to the top decile of recipient establishments. One important factor accounting for this was the scale of payments made to the shipbuilding industry. For RDG, 59.0 per cent of expenditure was accounted for by the top decile, while the figure for NSA was 61.4 per cent. The degree of concentration of local authority assistance was surprisingly high, with half the aid going to the top decile. This was despite the fact that their policies are generally based on spreading small resources over a large number of establishments. The *average* level of local authority assistance has been low, but the distribution is skewed such that a small number of establishments have, in fact, accounted for a disproportionate share of expenditure. Outside Tyne and Wear, the concentration of local authority expenditure was particularly high, mainly because Durham County Council has advanced a small number of quite large loans. Within Tyne and Wear, the level of concentration was lower but, even so, 46.2 per cent of expenditure went to the top decile (i.e. to 129 establishments out of 1290).

The pattern of concentration may be further indicated by identifying the largest individual recipients of assistance. Table 4.8 lists the ten largest recipients of DTI aid (these data are published; we are bound by confidentiality restrictions which apply to most of the data supplied to us by the other agencies). Over the whole period 1974–84, the establishments listed in this Table received altogether nearly £100 million. Many are well-known

Table 4.8. *The Ten Most Heavily Assisted Establishments by the DTI, 1974–1984* [a]

	Regional Development Grant	Regional Selective Assistance	National Selective Assistance	RDG, RSA, & NSA
1	Austin & Pickersgill[b] Sunderland £6 669 000 (Shipbuilders; nationalized)	Sunderland Shipbuilders[b] Sunderland £15 000 000 (Shipbuilders; nationalized)	T. I. Churchill Blaydon £776 000 (Machine tools; subsidiary of T. I. Group)	Sunderland Shipbuilders Sunderland £17 005 000 (Shipbuilders; nationalized)
2	Lombard North Central Leasing[d] £6 453 000 (Leasing Company; subsidiary of Nat. West. Bank)	Austin & Pickersgill[b] Sunderland £9 000 000 (Shipbuilders; nationalized)	George Blair[b] Newcastle £620 700 (Steel foundry; local independent company)	Austin & Pickersgill Sunderland £15 669 000 (Shipbuilders; nationalized)
3	British Steel Corporation Consett £5 322 000 (Steel works; nationalized—closed 1980)	NEI Parsons[b] Heaton £6 723 000 (Electrical & nuclear eng.; HQ in Newcastle)	Welwyn Electric Bedlington £583 528 (Electronic components; subsidiary of Royal Worcs.)	NEI Parsons[b] Heaton £6 976 401 (Electrical and nuclear eng.; HQ in Newcastle)
4	Federation Brewery[b] Gateshead £4 838 000 (Brewery; HQ in Newcastle)	Brentford Nylons Cramlington £5 301 000 (Household textiles; subsidiary of Lonrho; HQ in London)	E. Jopling & Sons[b] Sunderland £445 050 (Steel foundry; HQ in Glasgow)	Lombard North Central Leasing[d] £6 453 000 (Leasing company; subsidiary of Nat. West. Bank)
5	Scottish & Newcastle Brewery[b] Newcastle £4 249 000 (Brewery; HQ in Edinburgh)	Sterling Winthrop[b] Newcastle £4 220 000 (Pharmaceuticals; HQ in New York)	Bonas Machine[b] Sunderland £369 478 (Textile Machinery; local independent company)	Sterling Winthrop[b] Newcastle £5 658 000 (Pharmaceuticals; HQ in New York)

Table 4.8. *The Ten Most Heavily Assisted Establishments by the DTI, 1974–1984* [a]*—cont.*

	Regional Development Grant	Regional Selective Assistance	National Selective Assistance	RDG, RSA, & NSA
6	Alcan Aluminium Ashington £4 133 000 (Aluminum smelting; subsidiary of Canadian Co.)	Boots Cramlington £2 500 000 (Pharmaceuticals; HQ in Nottingham)	Davy Roll[b] Gateshead £277 462 (Steel foundry; HQ in London)	Boots Cramlington £5 444 000 (Pharmaceuticals; HQ in Nottingham)
7	National Smokeless Fuels[b] Jarrow £3 621 000 (Coke works; subsidiary of NCB)	Coles Cranes[b] Sunderland £2 443 600 (Manufacture of cranes and lifting gear; HQ in London)	NEI Parsons[b] Heaton £253 401 (Electrical and nuclear eng.; HQ in Newcastle)	British Steel Corporation Conset £5 322 000 (Steel works; nationalized—closed 1980)
8	NEI[b c] Newcastle £3 403 000 (Multi-plant engineering co.; HQ in Newcastle)	Plessey[b] South Shields £1 900 000 (Manufacture of printed circuit boards; HQ in Essex)	British Engines[b] Newcastle £230 632 (Precision engineering; local independent company)	Brentford Nylons Cramlington £5 301 428 (Household textiles; subsidiary of Lonrho; HQ in London)
9	Boots Cramlington £2 944 000 (Pharmaceuticals; HQ in Nottingham)	NEI, Clarke Chapman[b] Gateshead £1 777 560 (Marine engineering; HQ in Newcastle)	Whitley Bay Meat Supply Whitley Bay £181 819 (Wholesale meat suppliers; local independent company)	Federation Brewery[b] Gateshead £5 838 000 (Brewery, HQ in Newcastle)

10	Vaux Breweries[b] Sunderland £2 655 000 (Brewery; HQ in Sunderland)	Vickers[b] Newcastle £1 597 320 (Armaments manufacure; HQ in London)	Victor Products Wallsend £138 460 (Mining equipment; local independent company)	Scottish & Newcastle Brewery[b] Newcastle £4 262 000 (Brewery; HQ in Edinburgh)
TOTAL	£44 287 000[c]	£50 462 908	£3 876 530	£76 928 829
% OF KNOWN EXPENDITURE	26.7	58.5	70.6	29.8

Note: The details on activity and ownership shown in the Table relate to the position around 1983/4.

[a] Includes only published amounts; in the case of RDG these are payments greater than £25 000 and in the case of RSA and NSA approvals above £5 000. However, it is estimated that published amounts account for 79% of total expenditure on these three schemes (see Table 4.1).

[b] Denotes establishments located in the designated inner areas.

[c] Because of the manner in which the figures were published, this expenditure could not be allocated to any particular establishment of NEI.

[d] The ultimate beneficiaries of RDG claimed by North Central Leasing are not known, and so payments made to this company could not be ascribed to any particular policy area.

Source: *British Business*

companies and there is some overlap between the three lists of 'top ten' recipients. The 'traditional' industries are strongly represented (shipbuilding, engineering, breweries, and steel), industries which are generally capital-intensive and establishments which have experienced significant levels of investment.

Spatial Distribution of Assistance

Some assistance agencies/schemes operate throughout the study area, while others only operate in particular parts of the area. DTI schemes and the equity investment of BTG have been available throughout the Newcastle metropolitan region, and English Estates' rent relief has been widely available since English Estates' premises are on sites located throughout the area. On the other hand, Washington Development Corporation assists establishments only within the designated area of the new town and BSC(I) Ltd. has confined its operations to the steel closure area of Derwentside District. Local authorities only assist establishments located in their administrative areas. Urban Development Grant is generally only available in the D.o.E. designated inner areas and Enterprise Zone rate relief applies only to those located in the Zone.

The spatial distribution of assistance reflects these constraints on the operation of the different agencies/schemes. It also reflects, however, the spatial distribution of potential assistance 'clients'—in particular, the distribution of establishments engaging in investment. Furthermore, the local authority position is influenced by variations in the availability of powers and resources between the inner and outer areas of Tyne and Wear and between Tyne and Wear and the non-metropolitan authorities.

Patterns of expenditure in the metropolitan region

It might be expected that the spatial distribution of assistance would discriminate *against* the inner areas of the conurbation. The inner areas have, after all, experienced severe decline in their predominantly older, traditional industries while new industry has been mainly located on the periphery of the conurbation. However, this has not been the case. Indeed, the assistance system has been quite favourable to the inner areas of Tyne and Wear, principally because the industrial structure of these areas includes a significant number of large establishments in heavy industry which have attracted substantial amounts of DTI regional aid. This reflects the particular industrial geography of the Newcastle metropolitan region. Elsewhere, the pattern may be very different: the Glasgow study found, for instance, that inner Glasgow received a disproportionately *low* share of DTI assistance and the system strongly favoured the outer areas of the Clydeside conurbation (Lever and Moore, 1986, pp. 48–52).

Table 4.9. *Spatial Distribution of Assistance and Employment, 1974–1984*

	Tyne & Wear		Rest of study area
	Inner[a]	Outer	
Distribution of all assistance (%)	52	23	25
Distribution of total employment (%)	44	34	22
Distribution of manufacturing employment (%)	52	36	12

[a] D.o.E. designated inner area, as shown in Figure 3.5.

Source: *British Business* and relevant agencies.

The D.o.E. designated inner areas of Tyne and Wear received 52 per cent of total assistance expenditure over the 1974–84 period while having 44 per cent of the study area's total employment. In these terms, the inner areas thus received more than their 'fair share' of aid. Since assistance has been largely directed at manufacturing industry, it might be argued that the relevant comparison should be with the distribution of manufacturing jobs. On this basis, the inner areas received exactly their 'fair share' of aid: 52 per cent of total assistance went to the inner areas which accounted for 52 per cent of manufacturing employment in the metropolitan region (Table 4.9). Tyne and Wear as a whole, however, has received a rather smaller proportion of assistance than its share of employment—the County obtained 75 per cent of aid while having 78 per cent of total employment. It should be pointed out, in addition, that aid to inner area establishments has largely served to support the old industrial structure while assistance in the outer areas has more often promoted diversification through aiding the setting up of new branch plants.

Patterns of expenditure within Tyne and Wear

The spatial distribution of local authority assistance within Tyne and Wear is of particular interest since the Urban Programme is concerned with directing aid to the designated inner areas. Leaving aside expenditure on UDG, about 35 per cent of local authority assistance expenditure in Tyne and Wear is financed from the Urban Programme and this is aimed at supporting firms in the inner areas. Given this input of resources, it may therefore be expected that the inner areas would receive a favourably disproportionate share of local authority assistance. To examine this issue, it is necessary to look at the period since the introduction of the present Urban Programme in 1978 and compare the spatial distribution of local authority assistance against a suitable bench-mark. One bench-mark is the distribution of DTI assistance in Tyne and Wear, since it would be expected that DTI assistance, available throughout the study area, would not be biased towards the inner areas except in so far as it reflects industrial structure.

The results of this exercise are given in Table 4.10. Over the period

Table 4.10. *Distribution of Financial Assistance Expenditure Between the Designated Inner and Outer Area of Tyne & Wear by the DTI and Local Authorities, 1978–1984*

Policy area	DTI (RDG, RSA & NSA)[a]		Local authorities[c]	
	Total expenditure (£'000)	(%)	Total expenditure (£'000)	(%)
Designated Inner Area[b]	87 339	64.6	7 465	65.0
Rest of Tyne & Wear	47 765	35.4	4 013	35.0
TYNE & WEAR	135 104	100.0	11 478	100.0

[a] Unpublished RDG, RSA, and NSA apportioned according to the distribution of known payments.
[b] Inner area as defined by the D.o.E. and shown in Figure 3.4.
[c] UDG not included.

Sources: *British Business* and relevant agencies.

1978–84, inner areas of Tyne and Wear have, in fact, received a higher proportion of DTI assistance (64.6 per cent) than their proportion of employment, and this stems from the industrial structure, with some heavily aided industries in the inner areas (notably shipbuilding, engineering, and breweries). But the surprising finding is that within Tyne and Wear local authority assistance was no more concentrated on the inner areas than was DTI assistance (65.0 per cent of local authority aid went to inner area establishments, compared with 64.6 per cent of all DTI aid). In addition, the distribution of local authority assistance within Tyne and Wear has changed little over time, despite increases in Urban Programme funding for economic development: for the whole period 1974–84, 62.3 per cent of assistance expenditure in the County went to the inner areas, compared with the figure of 65.0 per cent for 1978–84. This issue—which bears strongly upon the question of the spatial targeting of policy—is further considered in Chapter 6.

Multiple Assistance

Finally, we focus on the *overall* operation of the assistance system, looking at the extent of overlap between assistance agencies/schemes and the incidence of multiple assistance for *each* agency/scheme. How far is it the case that establishments receiving aid from one source succeed in obtaining aid from another? Do the various agencies/schemes operate in different and distinct sectors of the 'market' or do they tend to assist the same groups of establishments?

Table 4.11 shows the incidence of multiple assistance to establishments over the period 1974–84. To take the example of RDG, the Table shows that, of the 412 establishments which have received (large) RDG payments, 251 (60.9 per cent) have received *only* RDG. 105 received assistance from one

Table 4.11. *Overlap of Financial Assistance Activities Between Agencies/Schemes, 1974–1984*

Agency/Scheme	No. of establishments receiving assistance from named agency/scheme						Total no. of establishments assisted by agency/scheme	% of establishments receiving aid only from named agency/scheme
	No Other	1 Other	2 Others	3 Others	4 Others	5 Others		
DTI RSA	141	125	69	15	0	2	352	40.1
DTI NSA	21	28	17	5	0	1	72	29.2
DTI RDG	251	105	44	10	0	2	412	60.9
Tyne & Wear District Councils	955	99	30	5	0	1	1090	87.6
Tyne & Wear County Council	124	49	18	9	0	0	200	62.0
Durham District Councils	29	4	1	1	0	0	35	82.8
Durham County Council	45	27	21	6	0	1	100	45.0
Northumberland District Councils	7	2	2	0	0	0	11	63.6
Northumberland County Council	34	2	0	0	0	0	36	94.4
English Estates	184	79	47	12	0	2	324	56.7
British Technology Group	15	4	4	1	0	2	26	57.7
Washington Devt. Corporation	172	31	9	1	0	0	213	80.8
British Steel (Ind.) Ltd.	74	31	14	7	0	1	127	58.3
TOTAL NO. OF CASES	2052	586	276	72	0	12	–	–
TOTAL NO. OF ESTABLISHMENTS	2052	293	92	18	0	2	2457	–

Notes: The Table includes only those payments for which details are known. An establishment may have been assisted by the same agency/scheme more than once over the period 1974–84, but this is included as just one case. Reading across the Table gives the number of establishments assisted by each named agency/scheme. However, care is needed when reading down the columns as there is an element of double-counting; e.g. there are 586 cases where an establishment has received assistance from two agencies/schemes over the period, but since each establishment is included twice in this column, there is therefore only half that number of actual establishments, i.e. 293.

Sources: *British Business* and relevant agencies.

other source over the ten-year period, 44 had aid from two others, and ten from three others.

Overall, the extent of multiple assistance is actually quite low. Of the total 2457 establishments which have received assistance from the sources listed in Table 4.11, 2052 (83.6 per cent) have had assistance from only one source. Multiple assistance will, however, be understated by these figures owing to the omission of data on smaller DTI cases. The level of multiple assistance does vary considerably between agencies/schemes. To examine the reasons for this it is first necessary to look at the structure of this overlap. Table 4.12 identifies the characteristics of this structure. Turning again to the example of RDG, the Table shows that the major overlap here is with RSA: 110 (26.7 per cent) of the RDG recipients have also had RSA (some have also had assistance from the other sources as well as RSA; the Table shows only the pairwise combinations).

The *lowest* levels of multiple assistance are to be found amongst the establishments assisted by Washington Development Corporation, Northumberland County Council, and the District Councils of Tyne and Wear and County Durham. This is because these agencies have primarily directed their limited resources towards helping small businesses, often new starters. Moreover, these establishments have, in many cases, been ineligible for DTI assistance, being in service industries, or because they were purchasing second-hand machinery, or were engaged in investment projects below the minimum thresholds.

Multiple assistance is more common amongst establishments assisted by Tyne and Wear and Durham County Councils. Again this reflects policy: Tyne and Wear County Council has tended to assist larger establishments, and provide larger amounts, than the District Councils, and these establishments have been able to obtain DTI aid. With regard to Durham County Council, the high level of multiple assistance derives mainly from the practice of assembling 'packages' of aid for firms, especially in Derwentside. These 'packages' may include assistance from DTI, English Estates, and BSC(I) Ltd. A little under half of the establishments assisted by English Estates, BTG, and BSC(I) have received multiple assistance. Many of those assisted by English Estates have also been aided by the DTI, especially from RSA. Both English Estates and BTG have operated throughout the study area and hence the group of establishments that they have assisted has also received assistance from a wide variety of other sources.

The *highest* levels of multiple assistance are found amongst those assisted by RSA and NSA. 211 (59.9 per cent) of the 352 establishments receiving RSA were aided from at least one other source, notably RDG and English Estates, but also, in several cases, from the local authorities. The high degree of overlap with RDG and English Estates aid appears to reflect the fact that RSA assisted establishments have often been incoming firms, receiving a negotiated multiple package of assistance from the DTI. NSA has the highest

Table 4.12. *Number of Establishments in the Newcastle Metropolitan Region Receiving Financial Assistance from Different Agencies/Schemes, 1974–1984*

Agency/Scheme		DTI RSA	DTI NSA	DTI RDG	Tyne & Wear District Councils	Tyne & Wear County Council	Durham District Councils	Durham County Council	Northumberland District Councils	Northumberland County Council	English Estates	British Technology Group	Washington Devt. Corporation	British Steel (Ind.) Ltd.	Total number of cases	Total number of establishments assisted by agency/scheme
DTI	RSA	141	22	110	45	30	2	15	2	0	68	7	11	12	465	352
	NSA	22	21	26	14	5	1	1	0	0	8	1	4	1	104	72
	RDG	110	26	251	26	21	1	2	0	0	35	3	6	3	484	412
Tyne & Wear District Councils		45	14	26	955	31	—	—	—	—	30	2	27	—	1130	1090
Tyne & Wear County Council		30	5	21	31	124	—	—	—	—	17	1	6	—	235	200
Durham District Councils		2	1	1	—	—	29	4	—	—	0	0	—	0	37	35
Durham County Council		15	1	2	—	—	4	45	—	—	27	3	—	37	134	100
Northumberland District Councils		2	0	0	—	—	—	—	7	2	1	1	—	—	13	11
Northumberland County Council		0	0	0	—	—	—	—	2	34	0	0	—	—	36	36
English Estates		68	8	35	30	17	0	27	1	0	184	4	0	29	403	324
British Technology Group		7	1	3	2	1	0	3	1	0	4	15	1	2	40	26
Washington Devt. Corporation		11	4	6	27	6	—	—	—	—	0	1	72	—	226	213
British Steel (Ind.) Ltd.		12	1	3	—	—	0	37	—	—	29	2	—	74	129	127

Notes: The Table includes only those payments for which details are known. Figures along the leading diagonal give the number of establishments assisted by just the one named agency/scheme. Other figures in the Table give the number of establishments assisted by each of the agencies/schemes named along the two axes. An establishment may have received assistance from more than two agencies/schemes; hence the figures in the Total cases column are at least as great as the figures in the Total number of assisted establishments column. Altogether the Table includes payments to 2 457 establishments.

Sources: *British Business* and relevant agencies.

incidence of multiple assistance cases (70.8 per cent of NSA recipients obtained aid from other sources); again there is a high degree of overlap with other DTI schemes.

The earlier analysis of concentration of expenditure for particular agencies/schemes pointed to a skewed distribution, with a small proportion of establishments accounting for a relatively large proportion of total expenditure. The same kind of distribution is to be found when *all* the assistance information is assembled on an establishment basis. *The top decile of assisted establishments has accounted for 84.2 per cent of total known expenditure* and the ten largest recipient establishments (which are also the ten largest recipients of DTI aid) accounted for 26.7 per cent of total assistance (£77 million out of £288 million known assistance). This concentration of assistance demonstrates, above all, the outcome of a system which is primarily based on subsidizing investment: the largest establishments, undertaking the largest investment projects, have received the lion's share of assistance expenditure.

An Overview of Assistance Expenditure

This chapter has looked at the structure of expenditure on financial assistance, using detailed information on payments to around 2 500 establishments over the 1974–84 period. It shows that a large proportion of the estimated £370 million spent on assistance has gone to support major investment projects in large-scale capital-intensive manufacturing industries.

The overall pattern of assistance is very much dominated by the DTI, particularly RDG which accounted for nearly two-thirds of total expenditure. Local authorities and other agencies represented a small, but growing, part of the assistance system. Like the DTI, the local authorities and other agencies have concentrated their efforts on manufacturing industry, even though over 60 per cent of employment is now in the service sector.

It is of particular interest to compare DTI and local authority approaches to assistance—and we examine this in some detail in the next chapter. Certainly, there are some key differences, not just in the relative magnitude of resources, but also such characteristics as the form and purpose of assistance. On the other hand, as we have seen, the spatial distribution of aid from these sources is similar, with some emphasis given to firms in the inner areas.

Having described the structural characteristics of assistance measures, the next chapter examines their impact and cost-effectiveness. This begins with a discussion of methods which may be used for evaluation and then, using survey information, looks at the effects of assistance on the operation of firms and the consequent impacts on the labour market.

5

The Impacts of Financial Assistance Policies

The data on assistance from the agencies themselves indicate the structure and characteristics of the assistance system and the agencies involved, but provide relatively little information on the *effects* of assistance. There are a number of ways of establishing these effects and impacts; we have chosen to use a survey approach. Questionnaire surveys of managers and employees of assisted firms have been used to explore both the impact of assistance on the operation of establishments and the implications for employment and the labour market.

The chapter begins with a discussion of the nature of policy evaluation and considers the different approaches and methodologies which can be adopted. This discussion makes reference to previous work and provides a context for our own study. This is followed by a description of the surveys, the findings from which have been used to explore key evaluative issues. The survey of managers shows which types of projects have been supported by financial assistance. We examine the scale of financial assistance relative to the input of resources from the private sector and explore, in particular, the extent to which assistance is actually necessary in ensuring that projects go ahead: how much public sector assistance expenditure is 'deadweight' (supporting projects which would have gone ahead in any case) or, conversely, 'additional'?

The managers' survey has also been used to look at the effects of these projects on the operation of assisted establishments and their employment. Reported impacts on employment have been analysed to consider the cost-effectiveness of assistance. This analysis provides some insight into the costs of different kinds of assistance in generating employment and takes into account the issue of 'deadweight' spending.

The last part of the chapter looks at the labour market impacts of assisted projects, drawing on data from a survey of employees at establishments included in the managers' survey. We attempt to identify the beneficiaries of the employment effects of assistance and, with reference to the concerns of urban policy, consider how far aid to firms in the inner areas leads to jobs for disadvantaged residents of these areas.

Policy Evaluation

The need for evaluation

Policy evaluation is of central importance in helping to ensure an efficient use of resources. To choose the 'best' among several policy options it is evidently essential to establish how well policies work—their impacts, the extent to which they met their objectives, and their real cost. Evaluation has become increasingly important, especially because of pressures on public expenditure, allied to a concern to justify policy in terms of its cost-effectiveness. The current importance of policy evaluation in the UK is demonstrated by the growing significance of the House of Commons Public Accounts Committee, the prominent role now played by the Audit Commission, and the evaluative work and policy reviews carried out within various Government Departments—D.o.E.'s evaluations of the Urban Programme, for example.[1]

Evaluation has a key role to play in the process of policy development and formulation. Even though expenditure may be tightly constrained, choices still need to be made; a local authority, for example, has to decide between different types of financial assistance and between expenditure on assistance, factory construction, or other measures. Information on the relative performance of different policies is essential in helping to make decisions, and a prerequisite for this is comprehensive information on the incidence and impacts of expenditure on policy measures together with a clear statement of objectives. In this study we have generally *not* found information on expenditure to be readily accessible and there exists a degree of confusion or contradiction about the precise objectives of policy. Finally, we would argue that evaluation needs to be a continuing, rather than *ad hoc* process, providing a way of continually monitoring and improving the effectiveness of policy.

Approaches to evaluation

An economic assessment of a particular policy measure should ideally embrace a full cost-benefit analysis of that measure to examine its desirability and compare it with other policy options (Pearce, 1983). However, there are several theoretical and practical difficulties involved in using cost-benefit analysis which make it difficult, possibly inappropriate, to apply to a scheme of financial assistance to industry (Grant, 1983). In the case of regional policy in particular, a lack of precision on objectives has compounded these problems and severely hindered attempts to evaluate the effectiveness of this policy (Armstrong and Taylor, 1985). Consequently, most studies of regional policy and other financial assistance measures have been of a partial nature, focusing on either the direct or Exchequer costs of policy or on the impact of policy on some specific economic variable such as employment or investment (Diamond and Spence, 1983).

Two key distinctions can be made in trying to categorize the different approaches taken to evaluation. *First*, the method of data collection: this can be either aggregate, usually published, data *or* detailed data for individual cases, most often obtained through surveys. *Second*, essentially three types of data analysis have been employed: shift-share analysis, regression techniques, and less complex statistical methods.

With regard to the use of aggregate data, the shift-share technique has frequently been used to establish what would have happened in the absence of policy (the 'counterfactual' position). This approach has been used, with various modifications, by Moore and Rhodes (1973, 1977, 1986) and others to compare the performance of Assisted and non-Assisted Areas when regional policy was active and when it was in abeyance (the 'policy off' period of the 1950s). Important criticisms have been levelled at this approach (Schofield, 1979). In particular, this method is likely to become less reliable as the 'policy off' period recedes further into the past. Moreover, to identify the effect of a particular policy instrument it is usually necessary to assume that other policy measures continue to operate with the same strength both prior to, and after, the introduction of the new measure.

Regression analysis has been used to compare the employment performance of Assisted and non-Assisted Areas (Weeden, 1974), but by far its most popular use in the regional policy literature has been to examine the relationship between regional policy and industrial relocation—this reflects the availability of data on the movement of firms (Ashcroft and Taylor, 1977). Regression analysis has also been used to examine the investment and employment effects of certain national sectoral aid schemes (Lambert, 1983; Gibbs, 1983). A general problem with this work—and with the shift-share analysis—is that is basically serves to indicate statistical relationships, but does not directly reveal processes.

The third approach has mainly involved the statistical analysis of data from surveys of those firms receiving assistance. This has been almost the only approach adopted by local authorities assessing their own assistance measures, reflecting, in part, their unwillingness or inability to undertake other forms of evaluation. A survey approach is also an obvious possibility since local authorities have access to their confidential data on cases they have assisted. Some academic studies have also been based on this approach (Barnes *et al.*, 1986; Turok, 1984), including an earlier study of local authority policies conducted in Tyne and Wear (Cameron *et al.*, 1982). Again, there have been criticisms of such studies; they have tended not to be comparative, in the sense that they have focused on a single measure, and to produce highly specific findings which may not be applicable to other situations and other localities.

The selected approach

Our own study has essentially been based on a survey approach, primarily so as to explore processes—how policies are seen to affect decisions and produce impacts. There are drawbacks with using surveys, not least the dependence on possibly unreliable responses. However, surveys do provide an opportunity to examine cause and effect rather than simply inferring a causal relationship, as with shift-share or regression analysis. The survey approach also allows examination of some central aspects of policy effectiveness, notably 'deadweight' spending and 'leverage'.

The detailed establishment data on assistance cases obtained from the agencies (see Chapter 4) provide an almost complete population from which to draw the survey sample of assisted establishments. A stratified random sample of those receiving assistance over the period 1980–5 was selected and managers were subsequently asked about assisted projects implemented over that period—five years was considered a suitable time-span to obtain reliable data on assisted projects and their outcomes.

An initial sample of 321 establishments, stratified by assistance agencies, was selected with the aim of interviewing managers at about 200 of these. In the event, 201 were successfully surveyed. The structure of the sample was geared towards achieving adequate numbers of cases assisted by the DTI and the local authorities to enable comparisons to be made between them. The 201 establishments were asked in the survey to identify the assistance they had received, and many had been assisted from more than one source. The 201 establishments included 127 which had obtained DTI aid and 119 assisted by the local authorities. Many smaller (unpublished) DTI cases, principally RDG recipients, were included, having been selected as known recipients of other forms of aid and then found to have also received small payments of DTI assistance.

To explore labour market impacts, a questionnaire survey of employees was carried out at establishments which had been included in the survey of managers. Questionnaires were completed and returned by 1388 employees at 120 of the assisted establishments, producing a response rate of 44 per cent. The questionnaire elicited information about the location of employees recruited by assisted establishments, their occupations, skills, and other characteristics to determine how the benefits of employment created in assisted firms are distributed within the labour market. This approach has been supplemented by analysis of Census travel-to-work data.

This methodology—this combination of methods—proved sufficiently robust to develop an assessment of assistance policies; we consider that it could also satisfactorily be used to undertake evaluation of other economic development policies.

The Role of Financial Assistance

In the first part of the survey, managers were questioned about the assistance they had received and the use to which it was put. In addition we discussed the importance of assistance in relation to total project cost and whether the assistance was actually necessary to ensure that a project went ahead.

Financial assistance may be considered in relation to those 'projects' which establishments have undertaken and which have been supported by assistance. Altogether the 201 establishments identified 254 projects which

Table 5.1. *Principal Purpose of Assisted Project by Agency/Scheme*

Principal purpose of assisted project	All projects		RDG assisted projects[a]		RSA/NSA assisted projects[a]		LA assisted projects[a]	
	No.	%	No.	%	No.	%	No.	%
Start-up of branch establishment	10	4.5	6	5.1	5	12.8	3	2.7
Start-up of new company	47	21.3	14	11.9	9	23.1	40	34.8
Acquisition of plant, machinery or equipment	95	43.0	70	59.3	9	23.1	30	26.1
Construction of building	6	2.7	7	5.9	2	5.1	5	4.3
Alteration to premises	10	4.5	5	4.2	2	5.1	5	4.3
Environmental improvement to premises	5	2.3	—	0.0	—	0.0	5	4.3
Change of premises	22	9.9	7	5.9	3	7.8	16	13.9
Product/business development	13	5.9	6	5.1	7	17.9	2	1.8
Others[b]	13	5.9	3	2.6	2	5.1	9	7.8
Not specified	33	—	11	—	13	—	15	—
TOTAL	254	100.0	129	100.0	52	100.0	130	100.0

[a] These figures refer to the projects assisted from each of the named agencies/schemes. In addition, these projects may also have had assistance from other agencies/schemes (hence the total for all projects is not the sum of the figures shown for the three agencies/schemes).

[b] Includes categories such as repairs to machinery, hiring of labour, business support, works to land, and the acquisition of existing businesses.

Source: Survey of (201) assisted establishments, 1985.

had received assistance from one or more agency/scheme. These projects received over £9.7 million public sector assistance, including £5.3 million in RDG, £2.2 million from RSA or NSA, and £1.4 million from the local authorities. Some projects have been funded from several sources; hence the 254 projects accounted for altogether 375 separate *awards* of assistance.

Purpose of assisted projects

Managers were asked about the principal purpose of the assisted projects. 95 (43.0 per cent) of the 254 projects involved investment in plant, machinery, or equipment. A quarter (25.8 per cent) supported the start-up of a business; this could be the formation of a wholly-new firm or the setting up of a new branch of an existing firm (Table 5.1). Clearly, 'start-up' can also involve the acquisition of plant and premises—but here the *principal* purpose was identified such that start-ups were distinguished from these related purposes.

There are some notable differences between the projects assisted by the three sources identified in Table 5.1 The major difference is that local authority assistance and RSA/NSA are more often associated with start-up than is RDG; however, it is of interest to note that virtually all of the local authority assisted start-ups were new *companies* while about one-third of start-ups assisted by RSA/NSA or RDG were new *branches*. Nearly all (24 out of 26) of the newly established branch plants and new companies assisted by RDG and RSA/NSA were in the outer parts of the study area—thus stimulating job creation and diversification in these areas—while inner area aid has mainly supported existing economic activity. Local authority assistance policies have mainly been concerned with helping small and new businesses. The survey underlines the importance of RDG as a subsidy for direct investment by existing establishments, since nearly 60 per cent of RDG assisted projects were principally concerned with the acquisition of plant, machinery, or equipment, while the comparable figure for RSA/NSA and local authority assisted projects was about 25 per cent. All three sources of aid have been used to support premises-related projects, with significant local authority emphasis on supporting the relocation of existing businesses mainly into local authority factories. Business and product development was not often specified by managers as a principal purpose of projects, although it is more commonly reported for RSA/NSA cases than for those assisted from the other sources.

The contribution of public and private sector finance

One important current concern is the scale of public sector assistance relative to the private sector input and, related to this, the extent to which assistance secures funding from other sources.

In total, the 254 projects involved an expenditure of £32.1 million, of which £9.7 million came from public sector assistance, £18.9 million was financed from the internal sources of firms themselves, and £3.5 million was from external private sector sources (a third of this from the banks). On this basis, the ratio of private finance to public assistance was 2.31; in other words, £1 of public sector assistance was accompanied by just over £2 of private sector expenditure. The ratio of private to public finance (Table 5.2) was highest for those projects assisted by RDG (2.70), while there was little difference in the ratios for RSA/NSA (1.88) and local authority assisted projects (1.94). It should be noted that these ratios refer to total public finance and not just that from the stated source; many recipients of RSA/NSA, for example, will have been aided from other sources, principally RDG, and this will tend to reduce the private to public finance ratio for RSA/NSA assisted projects. If only those projects funded from *one* source of assistance are considered, those projects in receipt of RDG alone have a higher ratio of private to public expenditure (3.82) than do those supported only by RSA/NSA (2.25) or local authority assistance (2.04). The maximum contribution RDG could make to a project was (until the revisions in 1984) fixed at 22 per cent

Table 5.2. *Ratio of Private to Public Expenditure by Type of Assistance*

Agency/Scheme	Ratio of private to public expenditure		No. of projects
	Mean	Standard deviation	
RDG assisted projects[a]	2.70	2.30	110
RSA/NSA assisted projects[a]	1.88	2.06	43
LA assisted projects[a]	1.94	3.27	115
Singly assisted RDG projects	3.82	2.52	58
Singly assisted RSA/NSA projects	2.25	3.21	11
Singly assisted LA projects	2.04	3.71	70

Source: Survey of (201) assisted establishments, 1985.

Table 5.3. *Role of Assistance in Securing Funding from Other Sources*

Agency/Scheme	Those saying assistance helped in gaining funding from other sources		No. of projects
	No.	%	
All projects	51	20.1	254
RDG assisted projects[a]	20	15.5	129
RSA/NSA assisted projects[a]	15	28.8	52
LA assisted projects[a]	10	7.7	130

[a] Figures refer to the projects assisted from each of the named agencies/schemes. In addition, these projects may also have had assistance from other agencies/schemes.

Source: Survey of (201) assisted establishments, 1985.

in the study area, giving a theoretical private:public finance ratio of 3.55. This represents a lower limit, since a project may include expenditure on items ineligible for RDG support (thus, the survey figure for singly-assisted RDG projects was higher than this, at 3.82). Singly-assisted RSA/NSA and local authority aided projects, where assistance is often negotiable, had, on average, a comparatively lower proportion of private sector funding. However, it must be borne in mind that this does not mean that RDG is, necessarily, more efficient at 'levering' private sector finance since it is an automatic subsidy which does not have to be 'additional'.

Few managers reported that the provision of assistance actually helped them secure funding from other sources (Table 5.3). Of the 129 projects receiving RDG, only in 20 cases did managers feel that obtaining RDG helped them obtain funding from other (private and external) sources such as the banks. The proportion was significantly higher for RSA/NSA (15 out

Table 5.4. *Outcome of Project Without Public Sector Assistance*

Outcome of project without public sector assistance	Source of assistance		
	RDG assisted projects (%)[a]	RSA/NSA assisted projects (%)[a]	LA assisted projects (%)[a]
Projects which were not 'additional' (i.e. 'deadweight')	(52.8)	(23.0)	(57.7)
Project would have gone ahead using finance from the firm	20.2	1.9	22.3
Project would have gone ahead using finance from elsewhere	19.4	11.5	20.0
Project would have gone ahead, but in a different form (e.g. scaled down)	13.2	9.6	15.4
Projects which were 'additional'	(41.0)	(55.9)	(40.0)
Project would have been delayed	19.4	13.5	16.2
Project would have been cancelled	20.8	40.5	23.8
Project would have gone ahead at another establishment in the company	0.8	1.9	0.0
Other	3.1	1.9	1.5
Not known/not stated	3.1	19.2	0.8
TOTAL (%)	100.0	100.0	100.0
TOTAL NO. OF PROJECTS	129	52	130

[a] These figures refer to the projects assisted from each of the named agencies/schemes; in addition, these projects may also have had assistance from other agencies/schemes.

Source: Survey of (201) assisted establishments, 1985.

of 52 cases) but very low for local authority assistance. In only 10 of the 130 cases assisted by the local authorities did managers consider that the assistance had helped them obtain other finance; this is probably because local authority assistance is often on too small a scale to significantly influence the banks and also because DTI assistance (to generally larger projects) may be more often associated with a project which requires finance from the banks.

'Deadweight' spending

The provision of assistance does not necessarily mean that the assistance itself was important or vital to the project being implemented—it might have gone ahead without assistance.

Managers were asked to give their opinion—in hindsight—on what would have happened if projects had *not* received assistance from the various public sector sources (Table 5.4). Such an assessment is clearly difficult to make but does provide some indication of the possible scale of 'deadweight' spending. Here we have defined deadweight spending as referring to projects which would have gone ahead even without public sector assistance using finance from the firm, finance from elsewhere, or those which would have gone ahead in a different form (e.g. scaled down).

It should be noted that this definition of deadweight spending is open to debate, in particular in relation to those projects which would have gone ahead in a different form or been delayed in the absence of assistance. For the purposes of this study, those projects which would have gone ahead, but in a different form, without assistance have been included within the category of deadweight spending although, arguably, some of this spending may not be considered deadweight to the extent that it secures an increase in the quality or scale of a project. Countering this, however, projects which would have been delayed have not been included under the deadweight spending category—although the bringing forward of a project may not be considered as significant a gain as securing a project which, without assistance, would have been cancelled. In both cases, it is a matter of degree and interpretation, but at least the effect is, to an extent, to counter the inclusion of the one group by the exclusion of the other. Moreover, it is worth repeating again that there are, necessarily, difficulties with a survey approach since it relies on assessments by managers which may be difficult to make. We might expect managers to overstate the importance of assistance—and thus understate the degree of deadweight spending on assistance (on the other hand, managers might tend to underestimate the importance of assistance, attributing success to their own efforts). However, *relative* levels of additionality or deadweight associated with different kinds of assistance should be reasonably reliable since the research is comparable and does not examine just one type of assistance measure.

According to managers, many projects would have gone ahead even without assistance. As shown is Table 5.4, more than half (52.8 per cent) of the projects receiving RDG would have reportedly gone ahead even without assistance (20.2 per cent would have used finance from the firm, 19.4 per cent would have been financed from other sources, and 13.2 per cent of projects would have gone ahead but in a different form). The same outcome would have occurred in respect of 23.0 per cent of the RSA and NSA cases and 57.7 per cent of the projects assisted by the local authorities. The survey therefore points to a much higher level of deadweight spending in projects assisted by RDG and the local authorities than for those projects assisted by RSA/NSA.

The levels of deadweight associated with RDG and local authority supported projects revealed by our survey are, in fact, similar to those found in a recent study of projects supported by the Urban Programme (JURUE, 1986b). In the absence of assistance from the Urban Programme, the JURUE study found that almost half the firms they interviewed would either have gone out of business or have cancelled or delayed investment projects. Other studies have confirmed the contrast between RDG and RSA/NSA. Allen *et al.* (1986) found that in 69 per cent of projects aided by RDG alone,

Table 5.5. *Percentage of Projects that Represented Deadweight Spending, by Source of Assistance and Purpose of Project*[a]

Purpose of assisted project[b]	% of projects, by purpose, that represented 'deadweight' spending		
	RDG assisted projects	RSA/NSA assisted projects	LA assisted projects
Start-up of branch establishment	66.7	40.0	(100.0)
Start-up of new company	71.4	33.3	65.0
Acquisition of plant, machinery, or equipment	52.9	22.2	36.7
Construction of buildings	57.1	—	(60.0)
Alteration to premises	(20.0)	—	(40.0)
Environmental improvement to premises	—	—	(40.0)
Change of premises	57.1	—	62.5
Product/business development	50.0	0.0	—
ALL PROJECTS	52.8	23.0	57.7

[a] A project is classified as 'deadweight' if it would have gone ahead in the absence of public sector assistance using finance from the firm, finance from elsewhere, or in a different form (e.g. scaled down).

[b] The categories outlined here relate to the principal purpose of the assisted project. Table 5.1 gives the exact number of projects within each category.

Note: Figures in brackets are based on less than 6 cases; figures are not reported where there are fewer than 3 observations.

Source: Survey of (201) assisted establishments, 1985.

the provision of RDG reportedly had little or no effect in ensuring that those projects went ahead. This was nearly twice the level of deadweight reported for projects supported by RSA—assistance was said to have had little or no effect in only 40 per cent of projects receiving RSA.

Purposes and forms of assistance

The issue of deadweight was further examined in relation to both source of assistance *and* purpose of project. The data are limited and in some cases there are only a small number of observations. However, there are indications that projects principally involving start-up (a new company or new branch) have a higher level of deadweight than other kinds of projects. Thus, for RDG, 66.7 per cent of projects involving the establishment of new branches would, according to managers, have gone ahead even without RDG assistance, as would 71.4 per cent of new company start-ups (Table 5.5). Similarly, for RSA/NSA and local authority projects the level of deadweight was higher for start-ups than for *all* projects assisted by these sources. For all three sources, the level of deadweight was higher for start-ups than for projects principally involving the acquisition of plant, machinery, and equipment.

In the case of local authority assisted projects, the high level of deadweight associated with start-ups seems directly related to the form of assistance given—often, rent or rate relief grants. These grants were frequently not crucial in enabling a project to go ahead—however, since the prime purpose of the aid may be to let a local authority factory unit, the level of deadweight might not be considered by the local authority to be important.

Effects of Assisted Projects on the Operation of Establishments

Managers of *existing* establishments (not new starts) were questioned on the effects of these assisted projects on their operations, in terms of increases in profitability, productivity, innovation, and sales. 168 projects were identified by these existing firms and it was reported that, in many cases, these projects had substantial beneficial impacts (Figure 5.1). 75 per cent of projects had resulted in increased productivity, 73.2 per cent in increased output, and 63.7 per cent in increased profitability. Many projects also involved an increase in market share (61.9 per cent), the introduction of new processes (54.2 per cent), or new products (48.8 per cent). These are outcomes which may generally be considered to be related to projects involving investment, the main focus for support from financial assistance. Fewer projects resulted in an increase in research and development (25.0 per cent of projects) or increased exports (19.6 per cent).

Differences in the effects of projects assisted by the three main sources shown in the Table are not very large; none the less it does appear that the kinds of projects assisted by the DTI are a *little* more likely to produce the kinds of benefits listed here than are the projects aided by local authorities. In part, this relates to the size of assisted establishments: the smaller establishments aided by local authorities are less likely to be significantly involved in exporting, for example. Overall, the findings are encouraging in that they do indicate that competitiveness, efficiency, and profitability have been increased through the implementation of many of these projects.

These findings do not, however, take account of the indirect effects of assisted projects, including local *displacement effects* on other firms whereby assisted establishments have been able to increase their market share at the expense of other local firms. To what extent do these projects, supported by assistance, benefit one establishment to the detriment of others in the area?

Displacement is difficult to measure, but the survey allows a limited examination of this issue through response to questions on market share and location of competitors (Table 5.6). Of the total of 254 projects, 147 (57.9 per cent) resulted in an increase in the market share of the business; of these, 69 had taken business from competitors located in the study area. The overall degree of displacement, indicated by the percentage of all projects which had

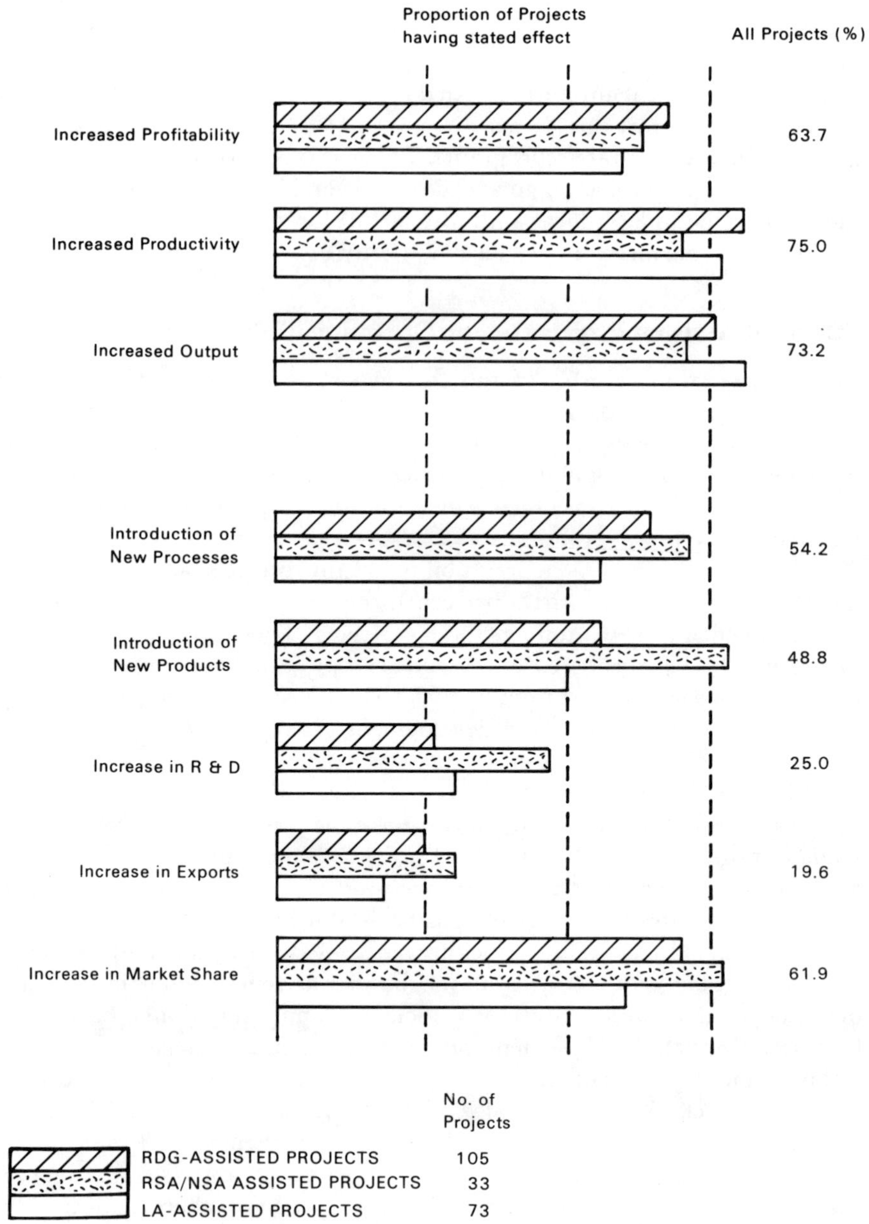

Fig. 5.1. Effects of assisted projects on the operation of existing establishments.

Notes: The figures refer to projects assisted from each of the named agencies/schemes. In addition, those projects may also have had assistance from other agencies/schemes. The figures exclude those projects where the principal purpose was the start-up of an establishment.

Source: Survey of (201) assisted establishments, 1985.

Table 5.6. *Displacement Effects of Assisted Projects*

	All projects	RDG assisted[a] projects	RSA/NSA[a] projects	LA assisted[a] projects
(1) Total no. of projects	254	129	52	130
(2) No. (and %) of projects reporting result to be increase in market share	147 (57.9)	89 (69.0)	39 (75.0)	72 (55.4)
(3) No. (and %) of those projects with increased market share taking business from local competitors	69 (46.9)	36 (40.4)	13 (33.3)	37 (51.4)
(4) Overall degree of displacement % ((3) as a % of (1))	27.1	27.9	25.0	28.5

[a] These figures refer to the projects assisted from each of the named agencies/schemes. In addition, these projects may also have had assistance from other agencies/schemes.

Source: Survey of (201) assisted establishments, 1985.

increased market share at the expense of local competitors, was 27.1 per cent and there was *little difference* between the groups of projects assisted from the three sources. Interestingly, local authority assisted projects were less likely to lead to an increase in market share than those aided by RDG or RSA/NSA. However, this difference is counterbalanced by the fact that the local authority assisted firms, being smaller and more locally orientated, were more likely to take any extra business away from local firms. The final outcome is, therefore, apparently little difference in displacement effects.

Employment Effects of Assisted Projects on Establishments

A large proportion of the assisted projects were reported to have directly resulted in the creation of employment. 137 (53.9 per cent) of the 254 projects led to a reported increase in employment at the assisted establishments and a further 37 projects helped in the retention of employment. 58 projects (22.8 per cent) had no direct effect on employment and only 5 (2.0 per cent) were said to have led to employment reductions (Figure 5.2). More of the RSA/NSA assisted projects involved increases in employment than did those projects receiving assistance from RDG or the local authorities. A relatively large proportion of RDG supported projects resulted in employment retention, suggesting investment which helped to maintain the viability of the establishment and so retain its current workforce. Many of the local authority assisted projects did not have any reported impact on employment. This could well be a reflection of the much smaller awards of assistance provided by the local

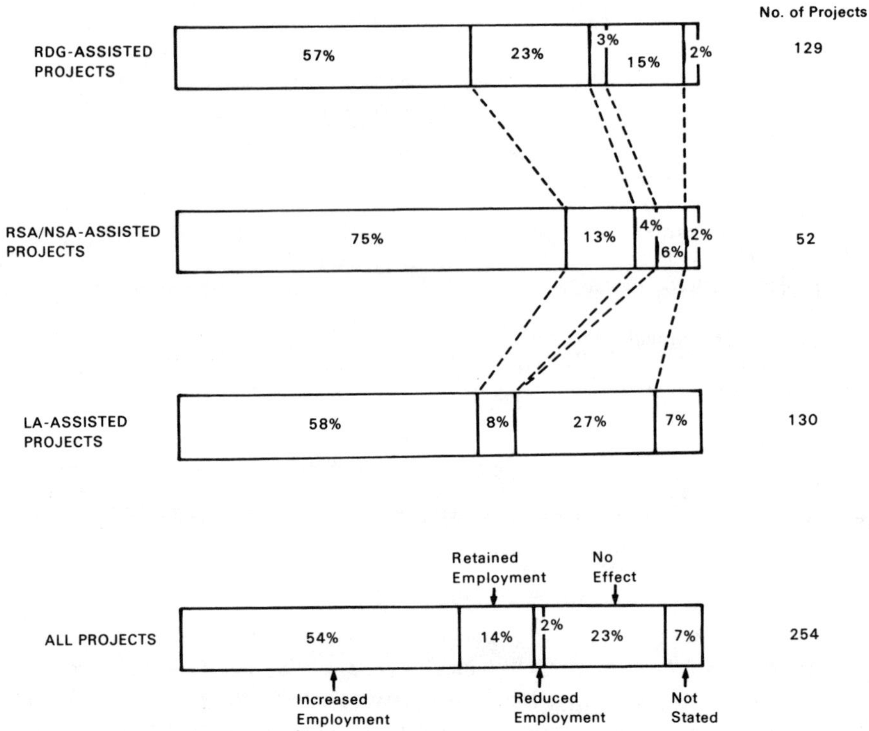

Fig. 5.2. Effects of assisted projects on employment.

Notes: The figures refer to projects assisted from each of the named agencies/schemes. In addition, these projects may also have had assistance from other agencies/schemes.

Source: Survey of (201) assisted establishments, 1985.

authorities in comparison with the other agencies, and also because many of these local authority cases involve assistance for premises (e.g. grants for alterations to premises, rent relief) which often do not have a direct employment effect.

The 137 projects which generated employment were reported to have led to the creation of a total of 1118 new jobs (715 for men, 403 for women). The majority of these jobs were for skilled and, to a lesser extent, semi-skilled workers, with only 5.5 per cent for unskilled workers (Table 5.7). A remarkably high proportion of these additional jobs were said to have been filled by people previously out of work (registered or unregistered unemployed). 794 (71.0 per cent) of the additional 1118 jobs were reported to have been filled by people out of work immediately prior to taking up this employment. Further information on the characteristics of employees recruited to establishments after the implementation of these assisted projects was obtained through a survey of employees; this is reported later in this chapter.

Table 5.7. *Characteristics of Employment Associated with Assisted Projects*

Outcome of project	No. of additional jobs	% of total additional jobs
Total additional male employment	715	64.0
Total additional female employment	403	36.0
Total additional employment	1118	100.0
of which:		
Jobs filled by those previously unemployed (registered or unregistered)	794	71.0
Types of jobs/occupations		
Extra managerial jobs	112	10.0
Extra clerical jobs	69	6.2
Extra technical jobs	70	6.3
Extra skilled jobs	433	38.7
Extra semi-skilled jobs	320	28.6
Extra unskilled jobs	62	5.5
Extra apprentices	25	2.2
Not stated	27	2.4

Source: Survey of (201) assisted establishments, 1985.

In this discussion of employment effects it is important to bear in mind that here we are referring to those jobs which managers said had been created as a result of the implementation of assisted projects. This should be treated with caution; it is important to appreciate that this does not imply that the assistance was necessary to ensure these projects went ahead and hence does not mean that the assistance 'created' these jobs. Moreover, employment gains from these projects form only one component of employment change—other events may have led to employment reductions in establishments, not least because these firms have been operating through a period of major recession.

The survey does confirm that there have been both gains and losses in employment. 195 of the 201 surveyed establishments supplied employment data for 1985 and, where appropriate, 1980. Of these, 100 had been in existence throughout the period, their total employment falling from 7403 in 1980 to 6359 in 1985 even though many had engaged in projects which had increased employment. The other 95 establishments had set up *since* 1980 and had provided a total of 1112 jobs by 1985; (but only 68 of these reported that their initial establishment—necessarily involving the generation of employment—was assisted and thus was identified by them as an 'assisted project' in the survey). The pattern is therefore a complex one—while assisted projects *have* resulted in the generation of employment this is not a net effect and it has been countered by job losses. Finally, it should be noted that the survey covered only those establishments assisted over the 1980–5 period which had actually *survived* to 1985.

The cost-effectiveness of assistance

One way of assessing the cost-effectiveness of public sector assistance in generating employment is to calculate the 'cost per job'—this is difficult, fraught with theoretical and practical problems. Here we can do no more than make a limited examination of this issue, indicating the relative magnitude of costs in relation to jobs created through the implementation of assisted projects.

In the employers' survey, managers were asked about the numbers of new jobs created in projects which had received assistance, and they gave details of the amounts and sources of assistance. From this it becomes possible to calculate a crude cost per job figure for all assistance, including those projects which did not lead to the creation of new jobs. However, this approach is of limited utility and it is possible to make some refinements. In particular, it is useful to take into account whether the assistance was 'additional'—that is, actually necessary to secure the implementation of a project—or represented 'deadweight' spending. In the employers' survey managers were asked to comment on the likely outcome if individual projects had not been assisted and this provided a way of distinguishing between 'additional' and 'deadweight' spending (see Table 5.4). Because some projects were multi-funded it was also necessary to consider the outcome in relation to each individual source of assistance and the analysis given below is based on this approach.

It should be noted at the outset that there are several ways of calculating cost per job (see Marquand, 1980) and that the measure adopted here, even though additionality is incorporated, is based on a fairly restricted definition. The survey excluded establishments which had received assistance and failed to survive. The figures take no account of displacement effects (that is, where jobs created in an assisted establishment lead to lost business and lost jobs in another establishment), nor do they take into account the multiplier effects of assistance within the economy (see Willis, 1983). Moreover, the analysis is focused on comparisons between existing policy measures and does not consider alternative ways in which the resources could have been used for job creation. Nor does it introduce the broader costs and benefits, such as savings to the Exchequer of reduced unemployment costs, or revenues in the form of taxes (Moore and Rhodes, 1975). Finally, the approach is quantitative (the number of jobs) rather than qualitative (skills, gender, conditions, etc.).

Table 5.8 shows cost per job calculations in relation to projects assisted from each of the three main sources (RDG, RSA/NSA, and the local authorities). It should be noted that each category, by source, covers all projects aided by that source—including those *also* receiving aid from other sources as well. A number of different measures are given to take account of deadweight and to deal with the problem of assessing cost per job when projects are multi-funded.

Table 5.8. *'Cost per Job' for Assisted Projects*

	'Crude' cost per job					'Refined' cost per job				
						Projects where assistance from named source was 'additional'		Projects where *only* the assistance from the named source was 'additional'		
	1	**2**	**3**	**4**	**5**	**6**	**7**	**8**	**9**	**10**
Source of assistance	No. of new jobs associated with projects assisted by named source	Number of projects	Total assistance paid to projects from named source	Total assistance paid to projects (all sources)	'Crude' cost per job (column 3) / (column 1)	Number of new jobs	'Refined' cost per job (column3) / (column 6)	Number of new jobs	Total assistance paid by named source	'Refined' cost per job (column 9) / (column 8)
RDG	593	122	£5 421 000	£8 287 000	£9 150	307	£17 650	72	£657 000	£9 100
RSA/NSA	522	48	£2 278 000	£6 614 000	£4 350	317	£ 7 200	112	£399 000	£3 550
Local Authority	567	123	£1 366 000	£3 459 000	£2 400	157	£ 8 700	93	£201 000	£2 150

Notes: All assistance figures are cost prices.

Projects receiving assistance from named source (RDG; RSA/NSA; Local Authorities) may also have been assisted from other sources.

In columns 6–10, projects where assistance was 'additional' refers to those projects which managers said would have been delayed, cancelled, or have taken place elsewhere had assistance not been given.

The cost per job figures in column 7 include all assistance from the named source but only the jobs in those assisted projects which managers said depended upon the provision of assistance, and therefore include some deadweight spending. Column 10 includes *only* the expenditure and the jobs created in projects where the named source was additional and therefore does *not* include deadweight spending.

The number of projects for which the cost per figures in column 7 were calculated are 53, 31, and 52 respectively for RDG, RSA/NSA, and Local Authority assisted projects. For the cost per job figures in column 10 the respective figures are 23, 12, and 41.

Source: Survey of (201) assisted establishments, 1985.

The first column of Table 5.8 shows the total number of new jobs associated with the projects assisted from each of the three sources. In the case of RDG, 593 jobs were associated with 122 projects (column 2) involving £5.4 million of RDG assistance (column 3). Some of these projects were aided from other sources, hence, *total* public sector support to the RDG 'client group' amounted to £8.3 million (column 4). The crude cost per job in the case of RDG, calculated by dividing the total RDG assistance paid by the total number of new jobs was nearly £9150. However, this is a crude measure because it includes projects which were not 'additional' (i.e. where the RDG was not necessary to secure the implementation of the project) and also because some of the new jobs may have stemmed from assistance from other sources—of the total of £8.3 million paid to the RDG 'client group', 36 per cent came from sources other than RDG.

In the case of the RSA/NSA projects, 522 new jobs were associated with projects receiving altogether £2.3 million RSA/NSA, giving a crude cost per job of over £4350—about half the comparable figure for RDG. The local authority crude cost per job figure was well below this, at £2400. However, both the RSA/NSA and local authority assisted projects attracted substantial proportions of assistance from other sources—much higher than was the case for the RDG group.

Columns 6 to 10 of Table 5.8 refer to projects where assistance was 'additional'. Column 6 shows the number of new jobs associated with those projects where the stated source of aid was 'additional'; thus 307 of the 593 jobs associated with RDG assisted projects were created in projects which were said to have depended on the provision of RDG assistance. On this basis 'refined' cost per job figures were calculated and are shown in column 7. Because 'non-additional' jobs are excluded, these cost per job figures are higher than the crude figures (in column 5). RDG is again shown to have a relatively high cost per job figure. The differences between RSA/NSA and local authority costs are reduced and reversed because of the large proportion of discounted non-additional jobs in local authority projects. But this has to be treated with caution since these 'client groups' may still have had assistance from other sources which was also 'additional'. The high proportion of total assistance expenditure accounted for by RDG also means that the cost per job estimate for RDG is likely to be biased upwards here.

The final part of the Table includes only those projects where the named source of assistance was 'additional' and thus here it is possible to attribute jobs more directly to the source of assistance (without the RDG bias noted above); in the main, these are single-funded projects. Once again, the cost per job figure for RDG projects is relatively high (£9100) in comparison with the figures for RSA/NSA (£3550) and local authority aided projects (£2150).[2]

The overall finding from the figures produced in this analysis is that the cost per job in RDG assisted projects appears to be significantly higher than that for RSA/NSA and local authority aided projects.[3] This contrast is shown throughout the analysis using a variety of methods. Other studies, looking just at regional policy measures, have found a similar contrast between the cost-effectiveness of RDG and RSA (Moore, Rhodes and Tyler, 1986).[4] The relatively high cost per job for RDG may well be related to the concentration of RDG on large capital-intensive manufacturing industries and it would seem that automatic capital grants which have not been conditional on meeting employment creation criteria are not the most cost-effective way of creating new jobs. On the other hand, there may well be good grounds for supporting large capital-intensive industries which are the mainstays of the area's economy and upon which many other local businesses depend. In addition, it is worth pointing out that projects assisted by RDG often help to secure the retention of existing jobs and assistance may, in some cases, actually be crucial to the survival of firms (McDowall and Begg, 1981).

Sector and size analysis

The survey data do not provide a sufficiently large number of cases to allow very detailed disaggregation but an attempt has been made to explore some of the factors (industry, size, and purpose of project) which may be relevant to differences in cost per job. Table 5.9 shows the 'refined' cost per job figures for each agency by industry (broadly, 'capital-intensive' and 'other' manufacturing industries) and by employment size group. Again, bearing in mind previous caveats and also the small numbers of cases, the evidence points to relatively high cost per job in the more capital-intensive industries and larger establishments. In relation to the industry categorization, the data show a consistent pattern for all three sources of assistance; the effect of this higher cost per job in capital-intensive manufacturing is particularly important with respect to RDG since a high proportion of RDG has been concentrated on these industries. In relation to regional policy as a whole, evidence from Moore, Rhodes, and Tyler (1986) also shows high cost per job figures in the more capital-intensive industries.

Cost per job and purpose of project

Examination of cost per job by principal purpose of assisted project indicates considerable variation between the different kinds of project, and the pattern of this variation is similar for all three sources of assistance (Table 5.10). Overall, cost per job appears to be highest for projects principally involving the acquisition of plant, machinery, and equipment or for the construction or alteration of premises. This is because many of these projects do not create new jobs; hence, the average number of new jobs reported to be associated with these kinds of projects is low. The data are limited, but it does seem that this holds for all three sources of assistance.

Table 5.9. *'Cost per Job' for Assisted Projects by Type of Industry and Employment Size Group*

Industrial grouping of establishment implementing assisted project	Employment resulting from assisted project, where either named source or at least one source is 'additional'	Public sector assistance paid to projects either from named source or in total (£'000)	'Cost per job' (£)[a]
Capital-intensive manufacturing[b]			
Overall	219	5 564	25 000
RDG	78	3 437	44 000
RSA/NSA	122	1 098	9 000
Local Authority	62	606	9 750
Other manufacturing[b]			
Overall	288	4 030	14 000
RDG	229	1 984	8 750
RSA/NSA	195	1 078	5 500
Local Authority	70	580	8 250
Employment size group of establishment implementing assisted project			
1–10 employees			
Overall	99	865	8 750
RDG	26	287	11 000
RSA/NSA	24	268	11 250
Local Authority	53	233	4 500
11+ employees			
Overall	433	8 860	20 500
RDG	281	5 134	18 250
RSA/NSA	293	2 010	6 750
Local Authority	104	1 133	11 000

[a] The 'cost per job' figures presented here are equivalent to those calculated in Column 7 of Table 5.8 and therefore include deadweight spending on projects where the assistance was not additional.

[b] Capital-intensive manufacturing industry referred to here are SIC Industrial Orders 3 to 10. Other manufacturing comprise the remaining SIC Orders in manufacturing (SIC Orders 11 to 19).

Source: Survey of (201) assisted establishments, 1985.

Table 5.10. *'Cost per Job'*[a] *by Principal Purpose of Project*

Principal purpose of assisted project	All projects		RDG assisted projects		RSA/NSA assisted projects		LA assisted projects	
	Ave. no. of jobs/project	Cost per job (£)	Ave. no. of jobs/project	Cost per job (£)	Ave. no. of jobs/project	Cost per job (£)	Ave. no. of jobs/project	Cost per job (£)
Start-up of branch establishment	(14)	22 000	(18)	12 750	(18)[b]	7 500[b]	(27)[b]	—
Start-up of new company	(6)	9 250	(10)	5 500	(12)	5 500	(5)	3 750
Acquisition of plant, machinery, or equipment	(3)	35 000	(3)	39 000	(4)	20 250	(3)	5 500
Construction of buildings	(5)	35 500	(5)	14 500	—	—	(6)[b]	15 000[b]
Alteration to premises	(3)	28 250	(2)[b]	97 000[b]	—	—	(3)[b]	3 000[b]
Environmental improvements to premises	(1)	—	—	—	—	—	(2)[b]	—
Change of premises	(3)	9 500	(4)	4 500	—	—	(3)	5 500
Product/business development	(14)	6 750	(14)	6 000	(19)	4 000	—	—

[a] The 'cost per job' figures presented here are equivalent to those calculated in Column 7 of Table 5.8 and therefore include deadweight spending on projects where the assistance was not additional.

[b] Denotes figures which are based on less than six projects; where there are fewer than three projects the results are not reported. The precise number of projects within each category is given in Table 5.1.

Source: Survey (201) assisted establishments, 1985.

Low cost per job figures were found for projects involving change of premises (many of these were assisted by local authorities and concerned moves to Council-owned premises) and for projects involving product/business development (largely NSA aided and often leading to the creation of a large number of new jobs). Of particular interest is the contrast between new branches and new company start-ups. The high cost per job of projects concerned with the *establishment of new branches* (£22 000 per job) seems to stem from the fact that, even though they create fairly large numbers of jobs, there is a relatively high level of assistance associated with such projects. *New company start-ups* have a similar level of deadweight to that of the branch plant projects and also have a high level of job creation: the difference is that the level of assistance is substantially lower and the cost per job is, therefore, also much lower at only £9250. This low cost per job may seem paradoxical given the earlier finding that a large proportion of the company start-ups would have gone ahead even without assistance; however, the point to bear in mind is that virtually all these projects do generate employment—and this contrasts with projects involving investment in premises, plant, or machinery which often do not create jobs.

Labour Market Impacts

The survey of managers revealed that many assisted projects led to an increase in employment at the surveyed establishments, creating job opportunities especially for skilled and semi-skilled workers; a majority of these new jobs were said to have been filled by those previously out of work (see Table 5.7). Here we look at these employment effects in more detail, examining the distribution of employment at the assisted establishments through the operation of the labour market. Given the emphasis in urban policy on the provision of employment for disadvantaged residents of the designated inner areas, it is important to determine the spatial distribution of benefits. In particular, to what extent do inner area residents benefit from employment created by assisted establishments located in the inner area? What are the characteristics of those employed at these establishments—are there differences between those employees resident in the inner areas and those from the outer areas? In short, who get the jobs?

To address these questions and examine labour market impacts, a survey of employees at assisted establishments was conducted. Establishments participating in the managers' survey were asked if they would also participate in a survey of their employees. 120 of the 201 establishments agreed and took part in the survey; 1388 questionnaires were completed by employees, a response rate of 44 per cent.

The survey involved the distribution, at workplaces throughout the metropolitan region, of a short self-completion questionnaire to all employees. The questionnaire elicited information about where people lived, their occupations, skills, etc. The spatial distribution of the 120 *establishments* surveyed was similar to that for the employers' survey, while the spatial distribution of *employees* covered in this survey (in terms of the location of their workplaces) was somewhat different, primarily because of the inclusion of a number of relatively large establishments in that part of County Durham within the study area. However, the numbers of establishments and respondents are adequate to support the analysis, allowing comparisons between inner and outer parts of the study area.

Inner area residents in the labour market

Table 5.11 shows some of the main characteristics of the employees covered in the survey, focusing particularly on those living in the inner areas of Tyne and Wear. The first part of this Table deals with *all surveyed employees* while the second part presents data on those employees recruited after the surveyed establishments had undertaken a project supported by assistance (*'post-project' employees*).

All employees Data from the employee survey showed that the inner area of the Tyne and Wear conurbation displays a high degree of labour market self-containment. Some 60 per cent of survey respondents living in the inner area worked at firms located in the inner area (Table 5.11). There was little evidence from the survey to suggest that *inner area residents* employed at the assisted establishments are more 'disadvantaged' than those employees living in other parts of the study area. The profiles of inner area residents and the rest of the study area were found to be broadly similar.

'Post-project' employees The rest of Table 5.11 focuses specifically on those employees recruited after the surveyed firms had undertaken a project supported by assistance in an attempt to establish the impact of assisted projects on the labour market. This approach is, admittedly, an imperfect way of identifying the beneficiaries of assisted projects, not least because recruitment is also a consequence of the normal turnover of an establishment. This group of post-project employees will only partly be coincident with the beneficiaries of assisted projects but it is the closest approximation we are able to achieve.

About half the employees included in the survey were recruited post-project. The characteristics of this group of post-project employees were found to be similar to the characteristics of the whole sample. A rather smaller proportion of post-project employees were men—this could well reflect the increasing proportion of jobs now being filled by women. 41 per cent of post-project employees said that they had been out of work immediately prior to taking their current job; this may be compared with that reported in the managers' survey—managers said that 71 per cent of new jobs created by

Table 5.11. *Characteristics of All Employers and Those Taken on Post-Project by Place of Residence*

Characteristics of employees	All employees		Post-project employees	
	Residents of Inner Tyne & Wear (%)[a]	Residents of the Newcastle Metropolitan Region (%)[a]	Residents of Inner Tyne & Wear (%)[a]	Residents of the Newcastle Metropolitan Region (%)[a]
Place of employment				
Inner Tyne & Wear	60	24	58	23
Rest of Tyne & Wear	32	30	32	22
(Total Tyne & Wear)	(92)	(54)	(90)	(45)
Outside Tyne & Wear	8	46	10	55
(Total)	(100)	(100)	(100)	(100)
Occupation grouping				
Managerial/technical	14	19	12	16
Skilled non-manual	23	18	21	17
Skilled manual	39	34	41	35
Semi & unskilled manual	24	29	26	32
(Total)	(100)	(100)	(100)	(100)
Percentage male	64	66	62	58
Percentage permanent	92	93	88	91
Percentage full-time	92	88	91	88
Previously unemployed[b]	—	—	48	41

[a] Percentages exclude not stated cases.

[b] The question of previous employment status was not addressed to employees recruited prior to 1980. The survey responses to this question therefore mainly comprise 'post-project' employees, hence a comparison of previous employment status between all employees and post-project employees cannot meaningfully be made.

Source: Survey of employees of (120) assisted establishments, 1985.

assisted projects were filled by people previously out of work. This difference may be partly accounted for by *under*-reporting by employees and *over*-reporting by employers, together with the inevitable inclusion of people who were recruited but not associated with projects generating employment. It seems reasonable to estimate that between 50 per cent and 60 per cent of employees recruited as a result of the implementation of projects were out of work prior to taking the job.

An analysis of data for *inner area residents only* revealed that, at least in terms of the main characteristics covered in the survey, people recruited from the inner areas following the implementation of assisted projects were no more 'disadvantaged' than the whole group of inner area respondents. This can be coupled with the earlier finding that inner area residents employed at the assisted establishments appeared to be no more 'disadvantaged' than residents from other areas.

Aid to inner area firms—labour market impacts

The survey data can also be analysed according to the *location of establishments (workplaces)* as opposed to the residential location of employees (Table 5.12). This makes it possible to focus on the relationship between the spatial distribution of assistance and the consequent spatial distribution of employment impacts. A particular issue of interest here is the extent to which assistance to inner area establishments provides jobs for disadvantaged inner area residents.

All employees The survey found that a large proportion of jobs in the inner areas were filled by people commuting from other parts of the conurbation. Of the total of 329 surveyed employees *working* at inner area establishments, only 113 (34 per cent) were inner area *residents* while 66 per cent came from elsewhere. In other words, there are substantial commuting flows into the inner area—although these are largely contained within the County, with nearly 90 per cent of inner area jobs filled by residents of Tyne and Wear as a whole.[5] Previously it was shown that the inner area is relatively self-contained, with 60 per cent of its employed residents working at inner area establishments. But it is clear that a large number of these jobs at firms in the inner areas are actually filled by commuters.

The employment characteristics of surveyed establishments in the inner area do appear to differ, in some respects, from the characteristics of the whole sample of firms. The evidence is not conclusive but the survey indicates that a lower proportion of jobs at the inner area establishments were for semi- and unskilled workers, perhaps reflecting the structure of the sample with the smaller inner area assisted establishments tending to have a higher skill profile.

'Post-project' employees Taking the 'post-project' group as providing a reasonable approximation to those benefiting from the creation of jobs in assisted firms, it is evident that commuting flows spread the benefits of jobs created in the inner areas to other parts of the metropolitan region. Only 37 per cent of the post-project employees working at the surveyed inner area establishments actually lived in the inner area. However, 90 per cent of the post-project group working in inner area establishments lived within Tyne and Wear as a whole.

In other words, post-project recruitment basically seems to follow estab-

Table 5.12. *Characteristics of All Employees and Those Taken on Post-project by Location of Assisted Establishment*

Characteristics of employees	All employees		Post-project employees	
	Establish-ments in Inner Tyne & Wear (%)[a]	Establish-ments in the Newcastle Metropolitan Region (%)[a]	Establish-ments in Inner Tyne & Wear (%)[a]	Establish-ments in the Newcastle Metropolitan Region (%)[a]
Place of residence				
Inner Tyne & Wear	34	14	37	15
Rest of Tyne & Wear	55	40	53	32
(Total Tyne & Wear)	(89)	(54)	(90)	(47)
Outside Tyne & Wear	11	46	10	53
(Total)	(100)	(100)	(100)	(100)
Occupational grouping				
Managerial/technical	22	19	9	16
Skilled non-manual	25	18	26	17
Skilled manual	37	34	49	35
Semi & unskilled manual	16	29	16	32
(Total)	(100)	(100)	(100)	(100)
Percentage male	70	66	59	58
Percentage permanent	96	94	95	91
Percentage full-time	93	88	90	88
Previously unemployed[b]	—	—	38	41

[a] Percentages exclude not stated cases.

[b] The question of previous employment status was not addressed to employees recruited prior to 1980. The survey responses to this question therefore mainly comprise 'post-project' employees, hence a comparison of previous employment status between all employees and post-project employees cannot meaningfully be made.

Source: Survey of employees of (120) assisted establishments, 1985.

lished patterns in the labour market, with a considerable amount of 'leakage' of benefits out of the inner area. In addition, the post-project data suggest that, in comparison with other parts of the study area, jobs provided at the inner area establishments were less likely to be for the semi- and unskilled and, related to this, were slightly less likely to be filled by those previously out of work. Nor was there found to be much difference, in terms of recruitment patterns, between the three groups of establishments assisted from the three main sources. Inner area establishments aided by local authorities, for example, did not generally recruit a larger (or smaller) proportion of employees, post-project, than those assisted by RDG. Overall, assisting inner area firms does not, by itself, appear to be a particularly efficient way of providing job opportunities specifically for disadvantaged inner area residents.

Policy implications

The preceding sections giving findings from the employee survey lead to an important policy point in relation to an urban policy involving assistance to inner area establishments. Assistance to inner area firms has conferred benefits on inner area residents—but generally only in line with existing labour market patterns. The spatial distribution indicates that nearly two-thirds of jobs created in the inner area assisted establishments were filled by commuters from elsewhere; and that, of the new jobs created, only one-sixth were for semi- or unskilled manual workers. Thus, providing financial assistance to inner area establishments without selecting those firms most likely to employ inner area residents, or without seeking to influence recruitment patterns, is not likely to improve upon established labour market patterns in distributing the newly created jobs. There is scope for improving the effectiveness with which financial assistance may be used to support and develop employment for disadvantaged inner area residents. This issue of targeting is considered further in the next chapter.

Notes to Chapter 5

1. Recent Government reports evaluating economic policy measures include the House of Commons Public Accounts Committee's reports on the D.o.E. Urban Programme (1986) and on Regional Industrial Incentives (1984); and the National Audit Office's reports on the Urban Programme (1985) and Enterprise Zones (1986). The D.o.E. has commissioned a series of studies evaluating aspects of urban policy—these include a five-year review of Birmingham's Inner City Partnership (PSMRU, 1985); an evaluation of environmental projects funded under the Urban Programme (JURUE, 1986a); an assessment of the employment effects of Urban Programme economic projects (JURUE, 1986b); and a study of the Urban Programme and the young unemployed (SAUS, 1986).
2. The cost per job figures presented in column 10 of Table 5.8 are lower than those shown in column 7, because they exclude deadweight spending on those projects where the assistance was not 'additional'.
3. The caveats expressed earlier in this chapter should be taken into consideration when comparing cost per job figures in this analysis. One of these caveats—the displacement issue—may, however, be of little significance since the survey did show that the degree of displacement may differ little between the groups of projects assisted from the three sources.
4. The cost per job figures for the regional policy instruments given in Table 5.8 may appear low when compared with figures given elsewhere. The 1983 White Paper (DTI, 1983), for example, gave a much-quoted estimate for the total

regional policy package of £35 000 (on average) for each new job created in the Assisted Areas during the 1970s. Moore, Rhodes, and Tyler (1986. p. 43), using the shift-share technique and aggregate data, obtained Exchequer cost per job figures of £25 000 for investment incentives and £17 000 for Regional Selective Assistance. In our analysis, however, the 'refined' cost per job figures given in Table 5.8, while including deadweight spending on projects which were not additional, are based only on those firms which received assistance and survived. Moreover, the figures do not take account of the displacement effects of assistance on both non-assisted firms and other assisted firms (the so-called 'domino-effect'; Deakin & Pratten, 1982). The figures presented in column 7 also do not allow for the multiple-funding of projects. Finally, it should be noted that the cost per job figure presented in the White Paper includes expenditure on the Regional Employment Premium, which has been shown to be a relatively costly method of creating new jobs (MacKay and Thomson, 1979).

5. The significance of commuting was demonstrated in a previous study of local authority policy in Tyne and Wear (Cameron *et al.*, 1982). This study found that only 41% of all jobs at inner area firms assisted by the local authorities were filled by people living in the inner areas. However, most commuters came from other parts of the Tyne and Wear County; 90% of these inner area workers lived in the County, only 10% commuted from further afield.

6

The Effectiveness of Assistance Policies

In the preceding two chapters we have examined the pattern of assistance expenditure, the effects that assistance has had on a group of surveyed establishments and the resulting impact on the labour market. This evidence is now drawn together and interpreted in relation to the problems of the area and policy objectives. We consider the *overall effectiveness* of financial assistance: what has it achieved and how could policy be made more effective?

To undertake a realistic assessment of assistance policies it is necessary to bear in mind the context within which these policies have operated. In particular, it is important to stress the scale and nature of the problems which policy aims to address—long-term economic decline, deep-seated structural problems, and high levels of unemployment. A fairly modestly resourced set of assistance policies cannot be expected to make an enormous impact on such substantial problems, especially in the context of a severe recession. Nevertheless, the resources involved (£370 million over the period 1974–84) have certainly not been trivial and policy has had some impacts; here we examine these impacts and consider whether *greater* benefits could have been derived had these resources been distributed *differently*.

To begin with, we look at the impacts of policy in relation to two key concerns: firstly, the contribution assistance measures have made towards strengthening the area's economy and, secondly, the impacts of these policies on employment.

Strengthening the Economy

The main structural problems of the economy of the Newcastle metropolitan region were previously identified in Chapter 2. These problems include:

(*a*) A continuing dependence, within manufacturing, on heavy, traditional industries in decline, coupled with an under representation of 'growth industries'.

(*b*) An externally controlled branch plant sector of the economy, vulnerable to the negative impacts of restructuring and poorly integrated into the local economy.

(*c*) An under representation of small businesses, a low rate of new firm formation, and an environment relatively unfavourable to the expansion of small businesses.

(*d*) Little growth in private sector producer services.

(*e*) A high proportion of the area's employment in the public sector, a sector under pressure from reductions in expenditure.

To what extent have assistance measures served to remedy these structural problems?

Sectoral patterns of assistance

The most striking feature of the assistance 'system' is that is has been dominated by subsidies for investment in manufacturing industry. The majority of assistance has come from the DTI, principally through RDG which supports manufacturing investment; in addition, the other schemes and sources of assistance have also been primarily aimed at subsidizing manufacturing investment. Altogether some 88 per cent of all assistance went to manufacturing establishments and only 5 per cent went to the service sector. Hence, with reference to the problems identified above, virtually all the expenditure and impact has been on manufacturing. Assistance policy has not been specifically directed towards the problem of little growth in private sector producer services (although, since the 1984 revisions to regional policy, some are now eligible for RDG). Nor has there been any focus on the public sector services which comprise a major element of the area's economy and employment; these are outside the purview of regional policy and there is no 'regional dimension' within public expenditure programmes.

Within the manufacturing sector, a substantial proportion of assistance has gone to industries which can broadly be characterized as 'traditional'—industries which are generally in decline both nationally and within the Newcastle metropolitan region. 79 per cent of assistance expenditure in manufacturing industry went to aid establishments in food, drink, and tobacco; chemicals; coal and petroleum products; metal manufacture; engineering and shipbuilding; and most of these industries have had high levels of assistance in relation to their shares of employment (Table 6.1). Traditional industries which are capital-intensive and have undertaken large investment projects have received a large share of assistance mainly because the system is dominated by automatic investment subsidies through RDG. Within the Newcastle metropolitan region, ten establishments have accounted for over a quarter of (published) RDG expenditure—altogether £44 million between 1974 and 1984. Nor is this situation at all unusual. In the Northern Region as a whole, three companies (ICI, BNFL, and BSC) received a total of £388 million in RDG over this period, about 44 per cent of the published regional total.[1] The degree of concentration of assistance is especially acute in the Cleveland (Teesside) area, where just two of these companies, ICI and BSC, obtained around 60 per cent of RDG provided to industry in Cleveland County between 1980 and 1984 (Foord, Robinson, and Sadler, 1985, p. 34).

In general, the assistance system has helped to support and maintain the existing dominant traditional manufacturing industries rather than particu-

Table 6.1. *Expenditure on Financial Assistance within the Manufacturing Sector, by Agency, 1974–1984*

SIC orders	Total known assistance from DTI, LAs, & others[a] £'000	Total known assistance from DTI, LAs, & others[a] %	% of Manf. Empl. 1981	Total assistance expenditure per employee (£)	% Assistance expenditure DTI	% Assistance expenditure LAs	% Assistance expenditure Others[a]
3 Food, drink, & tobacco	22 527	10.7	7.9	1 862	11.4	4.7	2.5
4 Coal & petroleum prods.	4 597	2.2	0.9	3 284	2.1	1.1	3.9
5 Chemicals & allied industries	23 434	11.1	6.0	2 547	11.8	6.2	0.8
6 Metal manufacture	16 666	7.9	3.4	·3 145	8.3	5.4	2.1
7 Mechanical engineering	37 112	17.6	17.0	1 416	17.6	15.5	18.6
8 Instrument engineering	1 321	0.6	1.5	574	0.4	3.0	3.1
9 Electrical engineering	20 844	9.9	14.1	961	10.0	4.9	13.2
10 Shipbuilding & marine engineering	40 268	19.1	15.0	1 743	20.7	3.7	0.0
(Subtotal)	(166 769)	(79.0)	(65.8)	(1 646)	(82.3)	(44.5)	(44.2)
11 Vehicles	1 448	0.7	1.6	603	0.4	3.9	2.7
12 Metal goods n.e.s.	4 658	2.2	3.4	896	1.3	8.5	14.2
13 Textiles	6 068	2.9	3.0	1 319	2.9	1.9	2.3
14 Leather, leather goods, & fur	36	0.0	0.1	180	0.0	0.1	0.3
15 Clothing & footwear	2 489	1.2	5.4	300	0.6	6.9	7.8
16 Bricks, pottery, glass & cement	5 966	2.8	4.5	865	2.8	3.7	1.7
17 Timber, furniture, etc.	3 371	1.6	3.5	624	1.0	8.8	7.1
18 Paper, printing, & publishing	10 554	5.0	7.5	918	4.5	15.3	4.9
19 Other manufacturing	9 801	4.6	5.2	1 210	4.2	6.4	14.8
(Subtotal)	(44 391)	(21.0)	(34.2)	(844)	(17.7)	(55.5)	(55.8)
TOTAL	211 160	100.0	100.0	1 370	100.0	100.0	100.0

[a] 'Others' comprise English Estates, British Technology Group, Washington Development Corporation, and British Steel (Industry) Ltd.

Sources: *British Business*, relevant agencies, and the Annual Census of Employment, 1981.

larly concentrating on (or discriminating in favour of) 'growth industries' or industries which might help to diversify the industrial structure. This generalization does, however, need some qualification: the chemicals sector in Northumberland, for example, does include some of the newer 'growth' industries in pharmaceuticals. It should be remembered that the period under consideration, 1974–84, was characterized by a significant reduction in mobile investment and, therefore, the opportunities to assist growth industries or diversify the economy were also reduced. This underlines the problems of operating a system most of which is *reactive* (it responds to investment) rather than *pro-active* (that is, directed at stimulating investment). In the absence of new incoming investment, it is clearly difficult to pursue a diversification strategy.

But while financial assistance may generally not be diversifying the industrial structure at the aggregate level it may be an important factor in strengthening the existing structure and this may include product diversification within existing firms in the area. The survey of managers did, in fact, point to substantial beneficial impacts on the operation of firms resulting from the implementation of assisted projects. Assisted projects often led to increases in the productivity, output, profitability, and market share of existing establishments and about half resulted in the introduction of new processes or products. These are clearly encouraging effects of the assistance system, particularly in a period of recession. Improvements in the operation of businesses help to strengthen the economy. Even so, it is worth restating that structural change—lessening dependence on traditional sectors—has not been achieved to any marked extent over the 1974–84 period through the operation of assistance policies.

This overview of the system as a whole does conceal some important differences between the agencies/schemes in terms of the sectoral distribution of assistance. Of agencies/schemes for which a sectoral classification could be determined, all have concentrated on manufacturing; however, the local authorities do differ from the others in that they have devoted a significant proportion (23 per cent) of their assistance expenditure to service sector establishments. Nevertheless, in relation to the *whole* system little assistance has been given to the service sector. Overall, only £12.3 million out of a total known expenditure of £240.1 million was given to establishments in the service sector, just over 5 per cent of the total.

Within manufacturing, the local authorities and other agencies have directed considerably smaller proportions of their assistance at 'traditional' capital-intensive industries than has the DTI (Table 6.1). 82 per cent of all known (published) DTI expenditure in manufacturing went to the traditional industries (food, drink, and tobacco; chemicals; coal and petroleum products; metal manufacture; engineering and shipbuilding). By contrast, only 44 per cent of assistance from the local authorities and from the other agencies went to establishments in these industries. In other words, local authorities and others have directed more attention towards the more labour-intensive, generally smaller-scale activities, such as paper and printing; 'other manufacturing'; timber and furniture; and metal goods manufacture.

With reference to the impacts of assisted projects on the operation of establishments, differences between agencies were not found to be very great. For the projects assisted from each of the three main sources (RDG, RSA/NSA, and local authorities) managers reported a beneficial impact upon the establishment in terms of profitability, productivity, and output in a high proportion of cases. One important difference which was indicated by the survey, however, was the relatively higher proportion of those projects assisted with RSA/NSA which resulted in the introduction of new processes and products, and which led to increases in R. & D., exports, and market share.

The distribution of assistance and the size of firms

Another important structural issue concerns the impact of assistance on *small firms* in view of the underrepresentation of small firms in the area's economy. Many of the economic development policy measures of the local authorities and other agencies have been aimed at fostering a higher rate of new firm formation, providing premises and advisory services. To what extent has financial assistance been directed towards the small firm sector?

It is difficult to provide an answer to this question because the evidence is very limited. The assistance data from the agencies are limited in two important respects. First, they exclude small RDG payments which would mainly have been made to the smaller establishments, and, second, the information refers to *establishment* size rather than *firm* size.

However, it does seem that, in relation to the assistance system as a whole, there has—at the least—been no particular bias in favour of the small firm sector. Within manufacturing, where the bulk of assistance has been spent and hence the sector for which a comparison is most meaningful, 61 per cent of all the establishments in the study area were in the size range 1–25 employees in 1978. By comparison, over the period 1974–84 only about 42 per cent of assistance cases were in this size range. Even bearing in mind the absence of small RDG cases from this data, there is no suggestion here of discrimination *in favour* of small establishments or, by extension, towards small firms.

Certainly in terms of the distribution of *expenditure*, rather than the distribution of *assisted cases*, there has been a high degree of concentration of assistance on large establishments, reflecting again the impact of measures supporting investment through proportional subsidy and the bias in favour of capital-intensive projects. This bias—which has concentrated resources on establishments and industries investing most heavily—is coupled with a bias within DTI schemes against small projects (and thus, small firms) through eligibility criteria which over the study period excluded very small investment projects and the purchase of second-hand machinery.

These comments refer to the system as a whole but do not take account of the very considerable differences between the different types of assistance. Local authorities and most agencies apart from the DTI do focus aid on small establishments and small firms, although the resources involved are relatively small in comparison with the DTI. 79 per cent of local authority assisted cases were establishments in the size range 1–25 employees and the proportions in this range were also high for English Estates (68 per cent), Washington Development Corporation (90 per cent), and BSC Industry (88 per cent). Comparable figures for the DTI assistance schemes were much lower: RSA (28 per cent), NSA (36 per cent), and *large* RDG payments (7 per cent).

The clear point emerging from this is that these other agencies have played an important role in reaching out to the small firms sector; in fact local authorities generally operate policies strongly biased towards this sector in acknowledgement of their limited assistance resources. But, by virtue of their limited resources, these agencies do *not* counterbalance the *overall emphasis* of policy, dominated by the DTI and focused on large investment projects and the large firms sector.

Impacts on employment

Clearly, the major problem of the local economy is unemployment. To what extent has financial assistance resulted in the creation or retention of employment?

The employers survey covered 201 establishments which provided details of 254 assisted projects altogether receiving £9.7 million of assistance from the public sector. Over half (54 per cent) of these projects resulted in an increase in employment and a further 14 per cent helped to retain employment (Figure 5.2). The 137 projects which led to increases in employment were reported to have produced a total of 1118 new jobs, mainly for skilled and semi-skilled workers.

There are severe difficulties in attempting to establish the *total* employment impact in the study area of *all* assistance expenditure on the basis of the figures derived from our survey. Cost per job figures calculated from the survey are almost certainly underestimates because the sample only covers survivors and takes no account of displacement effects. On the other hand, the figures take no account of positive secondary effects (e.g. on suppliers, and multiplier effects in the local economy), nor do they represent a net cost in that they are not offset against the costs of unemployment (e.g. transfer payments and 'lost' tax revenues).

With these caveats in mind we can, again, do no more than suggest an order of magnitude in terms of total jobs created. The refined cost per job figures excluding deadweight (i.e. column 7 in Table 5.8) may be used to calculate total employment impact by dividing the total expenditures from each of the three main sources by their respective cost per job figures. Over the period 1981–4, an estimated total of £136.7 million was provided in assistance to establishments in the Newcastle metropolitan region from these three sources. If this is related to the survey cost per job figures, it would suggest that this assistance in total supported the generation of an 'extra' 10 000 jobs over the period 1981–4. This would, however, be a substantial overestimate since no allowance is made in this calculation for the double counting of assistance in multi-funded projects, nor does it take into account displacement effects, other secondary effects, or non-survival of assisted establishments. The actual job generation effect might be as low as half this figure and this should be placed in the context of job losses over this period; between 1981 and 1984 total employment in Tyne and Wear alone is estimated to have declined by 38 000 (Tyne and Wear County Council, 1985).

It has been shown that the cost per job appears to vary by size of establishment, industry, and source of assistance (Tables 5.8 and 5.9). These differences are interrelated: for example, the high cost per job figure for RDG will reflect the often large expenditure required to generate jobs in large capital-intensive establishments. Overall, the figures suggest that the cost per job is lower in the smaller and more labour-intensive manufacturing establishments.

How cost-effective are the various sources of assistance as regards the generation of employment? RSA and NSA assisted projects were more often associated with increases in direct employment than were projects aided by RDG or by the local authorities (Figure 5.2). 75 per cent of RSA/NSA supported projects led to a reported increase in jobs compared with 58 per cent of RDG projects and 57 per cent of local authority projects. Few RSA/NSA projects had no employment effects (6 per cent) whereas the figure was higher for RDG (15 per cent) and substantially greater for local authority projects (27 per cent). RDG was, however, more often associated with job retention. In respect of cost per job, RSA/NSA and local authority projects were relatively cost-effective even though a quarter of local authority assisted projects had no employment effect. In general, RDG assisted projects incurred a much higher cost per job.

These findings essentially point to the benefits of a selective approach and the usefulness of linking the provision of assistance to employment creation, as is the case with RSA and NSA and, to an extent, with local authority assistance. Indeed, this may be regarded as providing some justification for the recent change in DTI policy which has now made the provision of RDG more dependent upon job creation. Moreover, a selective approach based on a recognition of the differences in the cost of job creation (notably by industry and by size) would imply a more cost-effective system and would serve to support efforts to strengthen the local economy through diversification and the encouragement of the small firms sector. On the other hand, it is important to note that there may well be good grounds for supporting large capital-intensive industries which are the mainstays of the area's economy and upon which many other local businesses depend.

Spatial Problems and Spatial Policy

High levels of unemployment are characteristic of most parts of the Newcastle metropolitan region, and reflect both the widespread incidence of job loss together with the commuting patterns of the area. Nevertheless, there is some spatial variation in residential unemployment rates. At opposite ends of the spectrum are the Ponteland area, with a 4 per cent unemployment rate, and Newcastle City Centre, with a 33 per cent rate (Figure 2.4). In relation to the zones identified in Figure 2.4, all the zones covering the older urban areas (designated as 'inner areas' for the purpose of the D.o.E.'s Urban Programme) recorded unemployment rates above the average for the area as a whole (19 per cent in March 1986). However, five other zones, outside the inner area, also had above-average rates of unemployment. High unemployment is principally—but certainly not exclusively—a problem of the inner areas. This pattern is repeated when other socio-economic indicators are brought into the analysis. Using a selection of eleven variables covering unemployment, employment, owner-occupation, car ownership, and school-leaving rates, all eight of the inner area zones are placed within the ten most deprived areas in the metropolitan region (Figure 6.1). Two non-inner areas are, however, within the worst ten: the vast housing estates of north-west Sunderland and also Consett in County Durham.

The various assistance policies are, to a varying extent, spatially focused, but the areas chosen for the operation of policy differ and represent a response to different concerns and objectives. Some policies are explicitly targeted on the inner areas, notably the D.o.E. Urban Programme. D.o.E. Enterprise Zone assistance in the study area also mainly covers the inner area. On the other hand, the DTI and English Estates have been operating throughout the Newcastle metropolitan region because the designation of Assisted Areas for regional policy support is based on the unemployment problems of whole labour market 'travel-to-work' areas. In addition, there are other agencies which focus their activities on particular localities: the local authorities necessarily operate within their administrative boundaries; BSC(I) has confined attention to the steel closure area of Derwentside; while Washington Development Corporation assists firms only within the new town designated area.

The spatial focus of policy only partly reflects variations in unemployment rates within the Newcastle metropolitan region. The largest component of expenditure, from the DTI, is spread across the whole area. The D.o.E., by contrast, has pursued a much more focused approach, with Urban Pro-

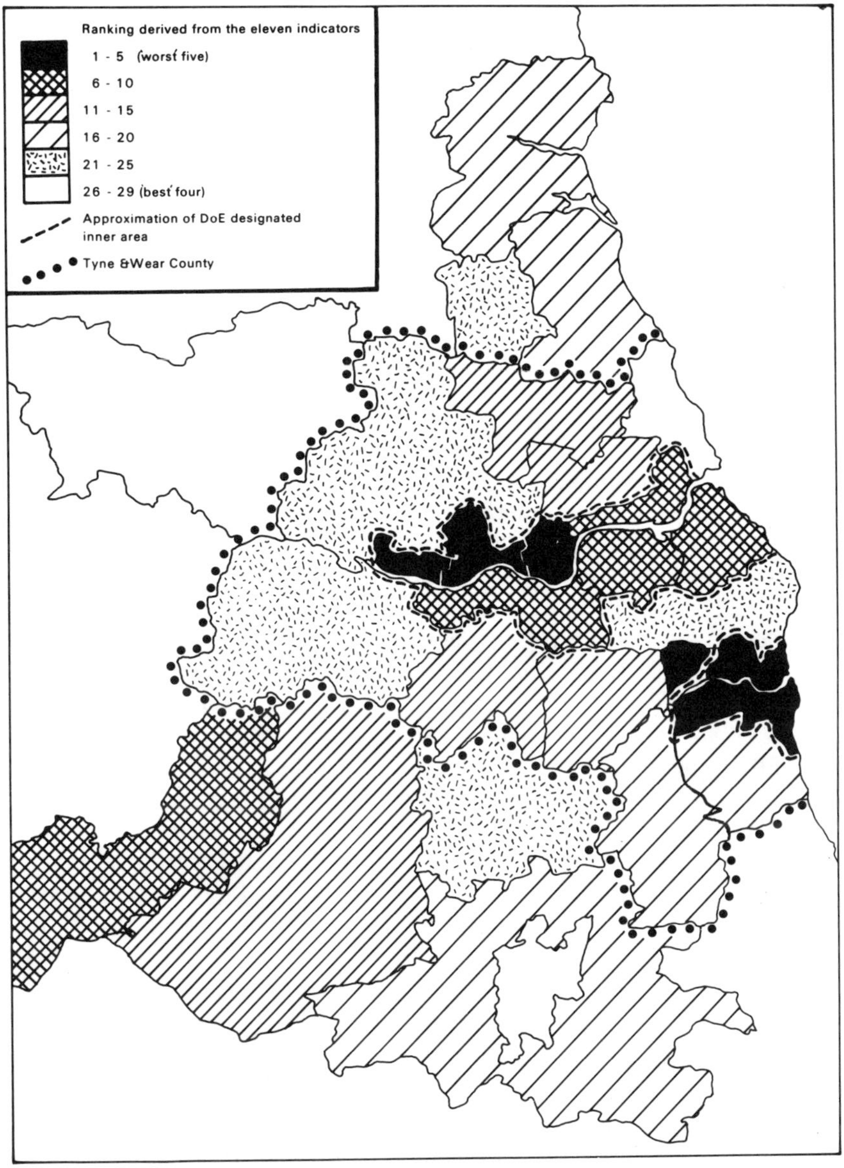

Fig. 6.1. Spatial variations in relative deprivation: areas ranked according to eleven socio-economic indicators.

Note: The eleven socio-economic indicators used were unemployment (total, male, female, 16–24 age group, 25–44 age group); level of skill of those in employment (semi-unskilled males, semi-unskilled females, blue-collar males); households not in owner-occupation; households without use of a car; and school-leavers aged 17. In calculating the overall index of deprivation, each of the eleven indicators was given equal weight.

Source: 1981 Census of Population.

gramme resources directed to the inner areas where unemployment is, in general, most severe. Washington Development Corporation and BSC(I) have both been concerned with 'outer area' localities; BSC(I) responding to a local problem of high unemployment, while Washington new town has been part of a 'growth point' strategy for the conurbation.

Policy and the inner areas

The D.o.E. approach has the strongest commitment to targeting in terms of the area and people towards which policy is directed. One of the prime objectives of the Urban Programme is to increase job opportunities in the inner areas, especially for disadvantaged people living in these areas. As regards *financial assistance measures* in particular, to what extent has this objective been met?

The Urban Programme is implemented through the Tyne and Wear local authorities, forming part of their economic development programmes. It has not proved possible to identify the Urban Programme components of assistance expenditure to individual establishments—primarily because local authorities themselves have not distinguished Programme expenditure on assistance.[2] These authorities implement policies which may be funded from various sources and draw on Urban Programme funding when the Programme's budget and the provision of the Inner Urban Areas Act enable them to do so—in this sense they tend to regard the Urban Programme as essentially providing one of the budget lines for assistance expenditure. Because Urban Programme expenditure on assistance is not separately identified, we have had to examine the incidence and impact of local authority assistance expenditure *as a whole* and in this way consider whether, in respect of this particular policy measure, the Urban Programme appears to have succeeded in biasing overall assistance expenditure towards the inner areas.

The incidence of expenditure Within Tyne and Wear, 65 per cent of local authority assistance over the period 1978–84 went to establishments in the designated inner area while 57 per cent of total employment (and 59 per cent of manufacturing employment) was located in the inner areas. There has thus been a degree of bias in local authority expenditure towards the inner area (Table 6.2). However, local authority expenditure was no more concentrated in the inner areas than was DTI expenditure as a whole; indeed, both RSA and NSA were *more* concentrated on the inner areas. DTI expenditure has been biased towards the inner areas because of the industrial structure of these areas; what is surprising is that local authority aid had a similar spatial distribution despite the contribution of Urban Programme resources (amounting to about 35 per cent of local authority assistance expenditure)

Table 6.2. *Assistance Expenditure and Employment in the Inner Area of Tyne & Wear, 1978–1984*

Agency/Scheme	% of total Tyne & Wear assistance expenditure in the inner area
RDG	62
RSA	71
NSA	74
(All DTI)	(65)
Local Authorities	65
Total employment	57
Total manufacturing employment	59

Source: Department of Employment and Relevant Agencies.

together with a policy commitment to discriminate in favour of the inner areas.

Jobs for inner area residents To what extent do inner area residents benefit from jobs created at assisted inner area establishments? In attempting to help inner area residents, the D.o.E. has sought to focus aid on inner area establishments—how effective is this approach? Moreover, are the benefits of policy reaching *disadvantaged* inner area residents?

The 1981 Census shows that a large proportion of inner area residents in employment work at establishments (in both manufacturing and services) within the inner areas; between 60 per cent and 90 per cent of employed residents in inner zones worked in the inner areas (Figure 6.2). Overall, three-quarters of the people living in the inner areas who are in employment work at firms located in the inner area. This appears to support the approach of targeting aid on inner area firms to benefit inner area residents. However, the Census also shows that a large proportion (58 per cent) of inner area jobs are filled by people commuting from outside this area. Of the 254 380 jobs at inner area establishments in 1981, 48 per cent (121 100) were filled by commuters from other (non-inner) parts of Tyne and Wear, and a further 10 per cent by people commuting from outside the County (Table 6.3). The employee survey displayed a similar pattern: 60 per cent of inner area *residents* in the sample worked in the inner area, while 66 per cent of inner area *jobs* were filled by commuters from elsewhere. The survey indicated that the spatial distribution of employees taken on after the implementation of assisted projects was little different from the overall distribution of all employees at these establishments (63 per cent of 'post-project' employees at inner area establishments came from outside the inner area compared with 66 per cent overall).

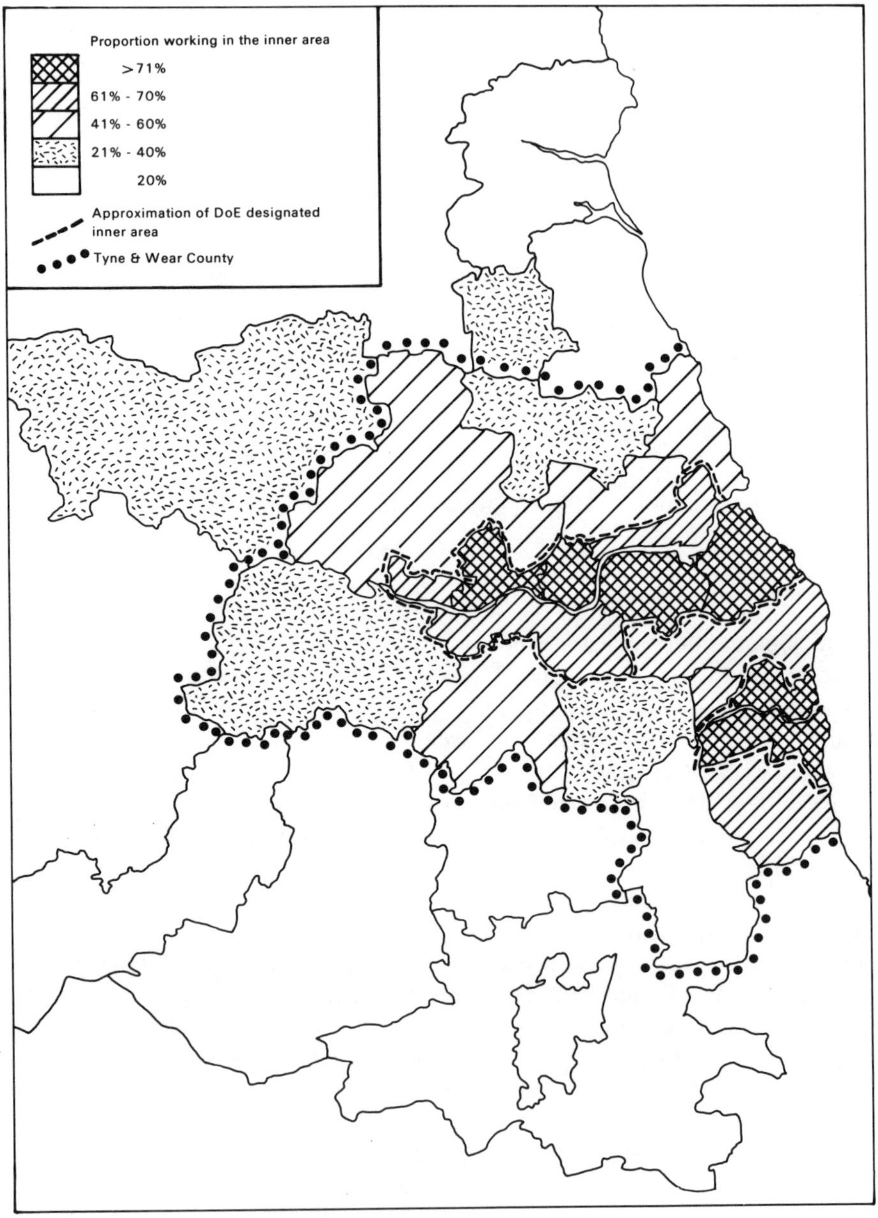

Fig. 6.2. Proportion of employed people living in each zone who work in the Tyne and Wear inner areas.

Source: 1981 Census of Employment.

Table 6.3. *Residential Location of Employees Working at Inner Area Establishments*

Residential location of employees	Jobs at establishments located in inner Tyne & Wear[a]	
	No.	%
Inner Tyne & Wear[a]	106 860	42.0
Rest of Tyne & Wear	121 100	47.6
(Total Tyne & Wear)	(227 960)	(89.6)
Outside Tyne & Wear	26 420	10.4
TOTAL	254 380	100.0

[a] The Inner Area referred to here is an approximation of the D.o.E. designated inner area. It is defined by an aggregation of wards and is shown in Figure 2.4.

Source: 1981 Census of Employment.

While these figures relate to establishments from all the agencies/schemes, there was little difference between them in terms of the creation of employment for inner area residents. Local authority assisted projects (including those supported by Urban Programme funding) were found to be no more likely to benefit inner area residents than projects supported by the DTI; moreover, two-thirds of the people recruited to inner area establishments post-project did *not* come from the inner area. The distribution of benefits from jobs created in inner area establishments appears to follow existing travel-to-work patterns—aiding these establishments has therefore not proved to be a particularly efficient way of targeting aid to inner area residents.

Nor do these policies seem to result in a bias in favour of the disadvantaged residents of the inner areas. The characteristics (skills, gender, age, employment position) of inner and outer area residents recruited post-project were found to be very similar. There was no evidence that the post-project inner area residents were more disadvantaged in respect of their position in the labour market than those from the outer areas.

We may conclude then that, despite the input of resources from the Urban Programme, local authority expenditure on financial assistance to firms is no more concentrated on inner area firms than DTI assistance. Moreover, many of the jobs created at inner area establishments are actually filled by people commuting from other areas and even those recruited from the inner area are not relatively more disadvantaged. So far as financial assistance is concerned, a much greater degree of control over targeting would be necessary in order to meet the D.o.E.'s objectives. Possible ways of improving targeting are discussed in the next section.

The Effectiveness of Assistance Policies: Performance, Problems, and Impediments

The need for a selective approach

The preceding discussion of the impact of assistance policy has indicated that there is a degree of inefficiency in the system and there is scope for improvement.

To begin with, there is a considerable amount of *deadweight spending*. According to the survey, over half the projects assisted by local authorities (58 per cent) and RDG (53 per cent) would have gone ahead in the absence of assistance; the figure for RSA/NSA assisted projects was much lower but still significant at 23 per cent. In total, 475 of the 1118 'extra' jobs associated with assisted projects were *not* dependent on assistance: according to managers, these projects would have gone ahead even without aid.

Moreover, the assistance system has not been very effective in dealing with the two major issues—strengthening the local economy and providing employment. Principally because most of the system has been reactive and non-discretionary (automatic subsidies on investment) it has served to maintain the existing manufacturing structure, rather than diversify it. In this respect it has achieved some success in increasing competitiveness and innovation; here again, the survey indicated that RSA/NSA assisted projects were the most successful. But assistance policy, at least over the period 1974–84, seems to have achieved little in terms of reducing the dependence on traditional industries, nor has it been directed at problems in non-manufacturing sectors which form a major part of the area's economy.

Assistance policy has had an impact on the generation of employment but there are substantial variations in cost-effectiveness. The greatest proportion of assistance has gone to large capital-intensive manufacturing establishments where the 'cost per job' has been greatest. RSA/NSA supported projects appear to have been most successful at generating employment (75 per cent of these projects led to an increase in employment, compared with 57 per cent of RDG and 58 per cent of local authority aided projects). In addition, effective cost per job was lowest for RSA/NSA and local authority assisted projects.

The generally reactive nature of policy, together with these indications of inefficiency, does seem to suggest that policy could be made more effective if operated more selectively, and the survey evidence on RSA/NSA supports this view. A selective approach could reduce deadweight spending; it would enable assistance to be more targeted at specific sectors and types of project; and would help to maximize employment creation. It is, of course, recognized that there may be conflicts between directing aid at, for example, 'new technology' industries and maximizing the employment impacts. However, to recognize this is to acknowledge the need for a strategy which directs assistance to particular economic activities, sizes and types of firms, and focuses attention on the scale and characteristics of employment which assistance to particular establishments may help to generate—selectivity therefore requires clear criteria by which to select projects and establishments for support. The need for a selective approach is perhaps most strongly and clearly supported simply by the prevalence of deadweight spending.

It is difficult at this stage to gauge the likely effects of the new criteria governing RDG, but it does seem likely that resources will be less concentrated on the 'traditional' manufacturing industries, notably the large and capital-intensive establishments. A few activities within the service sector have also been made eligible for RDG, but this is likely to lead to only a small reduction in the emphasis on manufacturing. These revisions to RDG have made it more directly related to job creation, but the problem of deadweight spending has *not* been tackled since additionality does not have to be demonstrated. Moreover, the new RDG assistance is still essentially *reactive*, reflecting the existing industrial structure and patterns of investment—rather than specifically seeking to promote economic diversification or respond to specific issues. Thus the revisions to RDG are to be seen as helpful in reorienting the assistance system towards job creation and away from subsidies primarily benefiting those industries engaging in large investment programmes which may create few jobs. But because RDG remains an essentially reactive form of support and the issue of deadweight has not been tackled, we argue that the findings presented here continue to be highly relevant to efforts to secure greater cost-effectiveness and a more efficient, directed, policy.

Targeting Problems of *targeting*—and, hence, the issue of selectivity—are central to the concerns of the D.o.E. in the Urban Programme. We have noted that aiding inner area firms results in a considerable 'leakage' of beneficial labour market effects to 'outer' area residents. The impacts of assistance are generally spatially distributed through the normal operation of the labour market without any particular discrimination in favour of inner area residents. To meet the D.o.E.'s objectives, including the concern to aid deprived inner area residents, a case can certainly be made for additional targeting mechanisms, or even for a totally different approach. A number of options might be considered:

(*a*) One method which might be adopted would be to tighten the criteria governing the provision of assistance such that establishments receiving aid through the Urban Programme would be required to recruit as far as possible from the target population (i.e. deprived inner area residents). This would have to be based on a clear specification of this target population. However, there may be some resistance from employers to such a scheme and potential employees may consider it inequitable.

(*b*) A second approach would be to assist selectively the kinds of establishments and industries most capable of providing employment for the target population (for example, assistance might be concentrated on inner area establishments offering lower-skilled jobs). There are problems with this approach: there may not be sufficient suitable applicants and such a policy would seem likely to conflict directly with a concern to promote economic restructuring.

(*c*) A third approach would be to assist the target population more directly through a wage subsidy scheme tied to this population. At present, the small-scale wage subsidy schemes operated by some local authorities do have certain eligibility criteria (e.g. the person recruited must be unemployed and in a particular age group). A similar scheme could be devised for which only inner area residents would be eligible. While it is acknowledged that wage subsidies may not be the most efficient way of promoting long-term employment creation in general, it may prove to be a more cost-effective method of providing employment for this particular target group.

(*d*) Fourthly, another method would be to concentrate efforts on the provision of training and retraining for the target group to help improve their chances of securing employment. While this policy may not directly create jobs it may result in some redistribution of employment opportunities.

However, more effective targeting implies effective monitoring mechanisms, not least to ensure that such criteria governing assistance are adhered to. At present most local authorities undertake little monitoring of assistance policies (in the course of this study it was found that some even had difficulty in identifying which establishments had been assisted) and there are few follow-up studies. Improvements have, however, been made to the arrangements for monitoring Urban Programme expenditure. Since October 1982, local authorities have submitted individual assistance awards for approval by the D.o.E. if they formed part of Urban Programme spending; prior to this the practice of submitting claims for block grant meant that Urban Programme supported assistance projects could not be identified. New arrangements, introduced in May 1985 under the Urban Programme Management initiative (D.o.E., 1985c), also mean that local authorities are now obliged to establish some limited forecasting and monitoring of outputs from Urban Programme projects (jobs created/preserved in the case of financial assistance). Arrangements must also be made to monitor individual projects in detail at least once in their lifetime.

The general absence of detailed information, coupled with little (if any) subsequent monitoring, is a widespread problem not just confined to the local authorities. The DTI, for example, found that it would have been very difficult to identify recipients of smaller, unpublished RDG payments—this was one of the main factors bearing on their decision not to supply such data to the study. On the other hand, some agencies did maintain adequate and accessible records. But follow-up studies of the impacts of such assistance were uncommon.

To increase the efficiency of the assistance system evidently requires both a selective strategy, to target assistance according to agreed objectives, and adequate monitoring, to ensure criteria are met. Monitoring is also a first step towards evaluation (which can serve to improve policy) and is necessary to maintain a coherent approach in a system involving a multiplicity of assistance agencies.

The need for a strategic approach

One of the most striking features of the current assistance system in the area is the large number of agencies and schemes: the DTI (RDG, RSA, NSA); 13 out of the 14 local authorities provide financial assistance; English Estates and Washington Development Corporation (rent relief); BSC Industry (loans and grants); Enterprise Zone (rate relief); and UDG. This list could be further extended—to include, for example, a variety of advisory agencies and certain MSC activities. Is this multiplicity of agencies a problem? What are the strengths and weaknesses of this situation?

If all the agencies were essentially doing the same thing, assisting the same firms, then the system would obviously be operating inefficiently. There would be a substantial duplication of effort and the possibility that firms could take advantage of the system, obtaining assistance from several sources each operating independently and unaware that others have aided a project. In fact, this does not seem to occur to any *great* degree. Table 4.11 showed that over 80 per cent of establishments assisted over the period 1974–84 received assistance from just *one* source (although this excludes smaller RDG payments). Moreover, where multiple funding (over the whole period and not necessarily for the same project) has occurred, this has often involved 'packages' of assistance such as RDG and selective aid from the DTI.

A system which, at first sight, may appear chaotic and involve duplication, actually seems to operate in a relatively well-ordered manner. Each of the agencies and schemes has particular objectives and aims to serve particular 'clients' and there does not appear to be a very great overlap between them. The evidence does indicate that the various agencies/schemes serve different 'markets', differentiated, most notably, by employment size, and also, in many cases, by location.

This differentiation may be considered a strength of the system rather than a weakness. While the DTI has generally focused on large establishments and large projects, the local authorities have concentrated mainly on the small firms sector. With regard to rent relief, the agencies involved (English Estates, Washington Development Corporation, and the local authorities) do not overlap since relief is granted to tenants of the 'client groups' they aim to serve, and this does suggest that in this respect they are complementary rather than in conflict. Furthermore, it does seem that the various agencies are well matched to the 'markets' they serve and the kinds of assistance they offer. Local authority industrial development officers are generally well placed to become informed about the small firms operating in their areas, the environment and needs of new firms, and are often able to offer a range of local authority support (e.g. premises, advice) or direct firms to other local small firms agencies. Similarly, those agencies, including the local authorities, which provide premises are best able to administer rent relief.

But it must be emphasized that, notwithstanding this complementarity, there is room for improvement. Above all, there is a need for a more targeted approach and this should involve not only improved targeting by individual agencies but improved targeting of the assistance system as a whole—since it is at this level that conflicts can arise. At present, because there exists a multiplicity of agencies with differing objectives, there is no coherent framework for action and therefore no concerted attempt at strategic targeting to address the problems of the metropolitan region. Each agency makes its contribution in relation to its own remit and perception of the problems rather than acting together to pursue an overall strategy; there is no agreed strategy to concentrate agencies' resources on, for example, specific sectors, areas, or groups within the labour market.

There is a regional policy and an urban policy and the two do not necessarily mesh together. D.o.E. urban policy aims to target assistance on the inner areas while DTI regional policy operates across the whole metropolitan region. As we have seen, DTI expenditure is very much larger than urban policy assistance expenditure and, hence, DTI expenditure determines the overall spatial distribution of aid. In the case of the Newcastle metropolitan region, the particular industrial structure—with some large capital-intensive establishments in the inner areas—does result in a concentration of DTI assistance in the inner areas. But this concentration is fortuitous rather than representing any attempt by the DTI to pursue an urban policy. Because of the relative scale of its expenditure, the DTI determines the pattern of aid and other agencies cannot significantly influence it. If, for example, the Tyne and Wear local authorities concentrated *all* their assistance expenditure on the inner areas this would make little difference: it would mean that 67 per cent of the total assistance expenditure of the DTI and the local authorities combined would go to the inner areas, compared with the current (1978–84) proportion of 65 per cent.

The first requirement is to establish an agreed strategy, involving a clear identification of the problems of the metropolitan region and the kinds of policies—and not only financial assistance measures—needed to address these issues. Conflicts between long-term structural policies, such as aiding particular growth sectors, and more short-term responses—targeting aid to support specific groups in the labour market, for example—would need to be resolved. It would evidently be necessary to establish the relative priority and, hence, expenditure to be accorded to helping areas of especially high unemployment, notably the inner areas, as contrasted with an approach to target aid at the unemployed throughout the area; if the latter approach were adopted and involved an effective targeting mechanism, it would actually result in a concentration of assistance in favour of the inner areas but would also reach other areas which have problems of a similar magnitude. Such an approach could also be used to focus assistance on other defined target populations (e.g. the unskilled). Moreover, the development of a strategy would highlight the need, and provide the explicit capability, of making trade-offs in terms of the distribution of scarce resources of finance and expertise.

Implementation of a strategy

To establish and carry out an economic development strategy it is necessary to have appropriate machinery both for policy co-ordination and implementation. At present, there is no suitable organization operating at the metropolitan region scale or at the broader regional level able to fulfil this role adequately. There is a notable absence of 'institutional capacity' at this strategic level. Within local government, the abolition of the Tyne and Wear Metropolitan County Council in March 1986 removed the most obvious candidate for such a role at the County level. In the sphere of central government, the regional offices of the DTI and D.o.E. are primarily concerned with the implementation of nationally determined policies, with relatively little scope for the *formulation* of policy and only limited possibilities to engage in the co-ordination of the economic development policies of different agencies. There are few economic development organizations placed between the 'local' and 'national' levels. Resources of finance and expertise are dispersed across a proliferation of agencies and there is no overarching forum to develop an overview of the region's problems.

The need for some kind of strategic organization is widely acknowledged in the North-East generally, and this need has been expressed, with varying degrees of urgency and enthusiasm, for several years. Politicians in this region tend to look particularly at the situation further north, envying the powers, resources, and autonomy of the Scottish Development Agency (SDA); a strong consensus has been built up that the Northern Region also needs an agency like the SDA, basically to compete for inward investment and to lobby for the region. Central government has resisted calls for the creation of an agency in the North with the extensive powers and major resources which are available to the SDA, remaining unconvinced that significant benefits would follow from the creation of another (expensive) 'quango', and also concerned that other English regions would demand the same treatment. The local authorities, together with the regional TUC and

CBI have, however, recently (early 1986) established a regional economic development agency, the Northern Development Company (NDC), and this has received some support from the Government. But the NDC, which presently has negligible resources, is very small-scale and limited in comparison with the SDA—although it may well grow and develop in the future. The local authorities see the NDC as an embryonic organization, subsequently to become like the SDA—indeed, a rival of the SDA—which would have powers and resources to invest in industry. The realization of such ambitions would, of course, depend on the future stance of central government. Certainly, it seems likely that the NDC will eventually acquire some important functions and some resources. It will probably subsume the North of England Development Council which is responsible for promoting the region as a location for the inward investment of foreign companies. The NDC may well eventually inherit some of the industrial development functions of the Washington, Aycliffe, and Peterlee New Town Development Corporations which are due to be wound up in 1988, and will have close links with English Estates. The main emphasis of the NDC does seem to be centred on competing for inward investment, providing a professional 'one stop shop' agency to comprehensively meet a company's requirements, and promoting the region with one voice—as was successfully done when a variety of agencies worked co-operatively to attract the Nissan car plant. There is, however, no suggestion that the NDC should have a much more extensive 'strategic' remit, encompassing and helping to shape the major economic development programmes of local or central government. The NDC, as presently envisaged, does not, therefore, provide the necessary machinery to devise, structure, co-ordinate, and implement a wide range of economic development policies.

Central government has become increasingly concerned to ensure policies are cost-effective and complementary, not conflicting; this, too, has led to efforts to establish more effective co-ordination. While the NDC is an initiative developed within the region and is to cover the five Northern Counties, central government has focused attention on improving the co-ordination and targeting of policy specifically in the inner urban areas by establishing City Action Teams (CATs) and 'Task Forces'. A CAT has been set up to operate within the Newcastle/Gateshead Inner City Partnership Area and consists of the Regional Directors of the D.o.E., DTI, and the Department of Employment and MSC. The intention is to provide an opportunity for these departments to co-ordinate their activities and develop priorities relevant to local needs, establish joint working arrangements, and monitor the outputs of programmes and projects. But while this initiative is to be welcomed, it is limited and could not provide the basis for the extensive strategic co-ordination which we consider to be necessary. The CAT does not embrace all the agencies involved in economic development—essentially, it only covers central government functions; and it only covers the Partnership area—it does not even include the Programme areas of the rest of Tyne and Wear.

The establishment of both the Northern Development Company and the City Action Team appears to demonstrate the recognition—by both local and central government—that institutional capacity is needed at a strategic level, not least to promote greater efficiency through co-ordination. In our view, the strategic machinery needed to carry out selective, targeted, and more effective economic development policies in the Newcastle metropolitan region would have to be much broader than either the NDC or the CAT, although it could usefully contain the main elements from both these models. Ideally, we would look for a strategy and an institution covering the whole metropolitan region, recognizing the labour market interdependencies in this functional region. To be effective, the strategy should include all the main agencies involved in economic development, drawing them into a coherent framework organized around functions (e.g. factory construction, youth training) rather than based on agencies and hierarchies (e.g. central/local government agencies and departments).

The multiplicity of agencies operating in the area is, on balance, a strength rather than a weakness in that they do have differing types of expertise, different client groups, and modes of operation. They are also mainly well-placed to deliver policy. They should be enabled to continue to fulfil their existing functions—but within an agreed overall strategy, their activities tailored to the needs identified in the strategy. The strategic institution we would envisage would not, therefore, seek to take over other agencies and their functions—in general, this seems unnecessary and would disrupt, dissipate, and even destroy the existing capacity to deliver policy. There may well be a case for a 'one stop shop' agency to handle all aspects of inward investment projects and this could be centred on the strategic institution (as proposed for the NDC). The question of which agency actually delivers policy is important—it is necessary to ensure measures are implemented at an appropriate scale, for example. But this is less important than deciding *which* policies to pursue and the *distribution* of resources between the different policy measures. To make policy more effective it needs to be coherent, recognizing interrelationships and potential conflicts, and it needs to be sensitive to local conditions; this implies a comprehensive strategy and an organization to ensure that the strategy is pursued, reviewed, and above all, remains relevant to the problems and concerns of the area.

Conclusion

The study has, necessarily, been limited in scope. We have focused on one particular kind of policy measure—financial assistance—and concentrated on one metropolitan labour market area. But, recognizing this, it can also be pointed out that financial assistance measures do represent a major component of the economic development policy 'system' and that the Newcastle metropolitan region does provide some important variations in terms of policy environments, notably between the conurbation core and the shire county periphery.

There is, undoubtedly, a continuing need for further empirically based evaluative studies of other policy measures (such as public sector factory construction or enterprise agencies) and of other localities. To establish—on the basis of hard evidence, rather than just opinion—what policy has actually achieved should be central to effective policy-making. Evaluation is no less important in efforts to 'defend' programmes than it is as part of an 'attack' based on 'cost-effectiveness'; in both cases, information is a vital part of the argument. We do not underestimate the substantial problems to be encountered in undertaking evaluation, having experienced them ourselves, but these problems can be much reduced, though not entirely overcome, by making monitoring and evaluation an integral part of the policy process. It is inefficient and inadequate to have occasional, isolated studies which have to start from scratch and spend a great deal of time collecting primary data: far better to incorporate monitoring into policy measures. The D.o.E. has started to do this through its new Urban Programme Monitoring initiative, and it is to be hoped that this is developed further to allow assessment of more complex 'outputs' than jobs created, floor space completed, and so on. Most of the other agencies involved in economic development policy have undertaken very little evaluation. Thus, despite the scale of expenditure, the DTI's regional policy is subject to little study other than generalized impact assessments based on aggregate data.

Evaluation would have a major part to play in building up the kind of economic development strategy that we have suggested is necessary; evaluative work would help to inform debate about alternative policies and consequent resource allocation. As we have shown in this study, there are detailed and complex choices to be made: financial assistance can be more or less cost-effective in relation to employment creation; it can be directed towards certain industries or size of firms rather than others; it can be aimed at subsidizing investment or wage costs. Empirical evidence helps to make these choices. Ultimately, however, the choices are political and thus hinge on questions of how the economic problems of the area are perceived and what the objectives of policy are.

It has become something of a ritual to point out that the objectives of economic development policy are difficult to uncover, poorly defined, often vague, and sometimes contradictory. In our view, it is important to establish meaningful (and measurable) objectives, not only to provide a framework for evaluation but also to show how a particular choice of policies is justified. Objectives can be vague and 'fudged' when only one agency is involved, setting out its own policies. But when several agencies are to be involved in a strategy—when it is necessary to agree and implement a co-ordinated series of policies—the statement of clear objectives becomes vital.

This study has shown that economic development policy may be based on a variety of objectives. At a general level, we have contrasted the objective of strengthening the economy with that of creating jobs. There is now a considerable gap between the two, particularly when investment promotes 'jobless growth' or even job-shedding. At the same time, distinctions between 'economic' and 'social' policy have become increasingly blurred—indeed, some would argue that a local strategy concerned only with economic development policy is too narrow and that it should encompass social policy issues as well.

Reflecting on the nature and scale of economic change in the Newcastle metropolitan region, one cannot avoid the conclusion that economic development policy has really had only a limited impact. Despite having had fifty years of regional policy assistance, the area still has major economic problems and remains significantly disadvantaged relative to the country as a whole. However, without such policy intervention, the situation would have been considerably worse. Central and local government economic development policies have helped to bring new industries to the area and assisted firms to modernize and survive; public sector agencies have also been very important providers of new factory premises, filling the gap left by the private sector. Large sums have been spent on financial assistance to industry and on a range of infrastructural projects in support of economic development—public expenditure which has obviously been welcome and has certainly been necessary to help the area cope with economic change. On the other side of the coin, it does need to be emphasized that, to a great extent, the area's economic difficulties have stemmed from decisions taken within the public sector—the run-down of steel, coal, and shipbuilding, for example. Ameliorative policies have clearly not matched the scale of these difficulties.

No doubt, much more could be achieved with a larger commitment of resources. But resources will always be limited—hence, it is not just a question of money, but also a matter of how it is spent. Having looked closely at how some of the money is spent, it seems clear to us that there is scope for improvement.

Notes to Chapter 6

1. Out of total published expenditure on RDG in the Northern Region between 1974 and 1984 of £879m. Imperial Chemical Industries received £154m. (18%), the British Steel Corporation received £125m. (14%), and £109m.(12%) was paid to British Nuclear Fuels Limited.
2. The D.o.E. has recognized the problem of identifying those local authority assistance cases actually funded from the Urban Programme. Since 1982 local authorities have had to identify Urban Programme supported assistance cases and seek prior approval for this expenditure from the D.o.E. Regional Office. In addition to this, the D.o.E. introduced new procedures in 1985 (the Urban Programme Management initiative) which now require local authorities to forecast and subsequently assess jobs created/preserved through assistance funded from the Urban Programme.

REFERENCES

ALLEN, K., BEGG, H., MCDOWALL. S., and WALKER, G. (1986) *Regional Incentives and the Investment Decision of the Firm*, HMSO, London.

ARCHBISHOP OF CANTERBURY'S COMMISSION (1985) *Faith in the City*, Report of the Archbishop of Canterbury's Commission on Urban Priority Areas, Church House Publishing, London.

ARMSTRONG, H. and TAYLOR, J. (1985) *Regional Economics and Policy*, Philip Allan Publishers, Oxford.

ASHCROFT, B. and TAYLOR, J. (1977) 'The Movement of Manufacturing Industry and the Effects of Regional Economic Policy', *Oxford Economic Papers* 29.

ASSOCIATION OF METROPOLITAN AUTHORITIES (1986) *Programme for Partnership: An Urban Policy Statement*, AMA, Partnership and Programme Authorities Group, May.

BARNES, I., CAMPBELL, J., and DAVIES, H. (1986) 'An Evaluation of Local Authority Financial Assistance to Small Firms', *Local Government Studies* 12.

BEAN, D. (1971) *Tyneside: A Biography*, MacMillan, London.

BODDY, M., LOVERING, J., and BASSETT, K. (1986) *Sunbelt City? A Study of Economic Change in Britain's M4 Growth Corridor*, Clarendon Press, Oxford.

BRITISH BUSINESS (1986) 'Revamped ERDF: How it works', *British Business*, 28th February.

BURNS, W. (1980) *Review of Local Authority Assistance to Industry and Commerce*, Report of the Joint Group of Officials of Local Authority Associations and Government Departments, D.o.E., July.

BUSWELL, R. J. (1983) 'Urban and Regional Policy: Assistance from Central Government to the Northern Region', in R. J. Buswell (ed.), *The North in the Eighties: Regional Policies for a Decade*, Regional Studies Association (Northern Branch).

CAMERON, S. J., DABINETT, G., GILLARD, A., WHISKER, P., WILLIAMS, R., and WILLIS, K. (1982) *Local Authority Aid to Industry: An Evaluation in Tyne and Wear*, Department of the Environment, London.

CHALKLEY, B. and PERRY, M. (1984) 'How Many Factories do we Need?, *Town and Country Planning*, February.

COOMBES, M. G., DIXON, J. S., GODDARD, J. B., TAYLOR, P. J., and OPENSHAW, S. (1980) 'Functional Regions for the 1981 Census of Britain: A User's Guide to the CURDS definition', *CURDS Discussion Paper 30*, University of Newcastle upon Tyne.

—— —— —— —— —— (1981) 'Appropriate Areas for Census Analysis: An Outline of Functional Regions', *CURDS Discussion Paper 41*, University of Newcastle upon Tyne.

COULSON, A. (1986) 'Section 137 in the Metropolitan Counties', *Local Government Policy Making* 12.

DABINETT, G. and WHISKER, P. (1981) 'The Declaration of Industrial Improvement Areas and the Provision of Advance Factories, Loans and Grants by Local Authorities in Tyne and Wear, 1974–79', *Inner City Employment Project, Working Paper No. 2, Department of Town and Country Planning*, University of Newcastle upon Tyne.

DEAKIN, B. M. and PRATTEN, C. F. (1982) *Effects of the Temporary Employment Subsidy*, Cambridge University Press.

DELOITTE, HASKINS, AND SELLS (1984) *Local Enterprise Agencies*, Greenaway Harrison Limited, London.

DIAMOND, D. and SPENCE, N. (1983) *Regional Policy Evaluation: A Methodological Review and the Scottish Example*, Gower, Farnborough.

D.O.E. (1981) *Enterprise Zones*, Department of the Environment, London, April.

—— (1983) *Urban Development Grant: Guidance Notes*, Department of the Environment, London.

—— (1985a) *Urban Programme: Ministerial Guidelines*, Department of the Environment, London.

—— (1985b) *Enterprise Zone Information, 1983–84*, Department of the Environment, London, July.

—— (1985c) *Urban Programme Management Guidance Notes (1–6) and Management Revision Note 1*, Department of the Environment, London.

—— (1986) *The Urban Programme, 1985: A Report on its Operation and Achievements in England*, Department of the Environment, London, June.

DTI (1983) *Regional Industrial Development*, Department of Trade and Industry, Cmnd. 9111, HMSO, London.

EVERSLEY, J. (1985) 'ENTRUST: Does a New Approach to an Old Problem Work?', *Northern Economic Review*, 11, 22–31.

FOORD, J., ROBINSON, F., and SADLER, D. (1985) *The Quiet Revolution: Social and Economic Change on Teesside, 1965–1985*, BBC, North-East, Newcastle.

GANGULY, P. (1984) 'Business Starts and Stops: Regional Analysis by Turnover, Size and Sector, 1980–83', *British Business* 2, November.

GARRAHAN, P. (1986) 'Nissan in the North-East of England', *Capital and Class* 27, 5–13.

GIBBS, R. (1983) 'Wool Textile Industry Scheme Stage II: An Econometric Analysis of Stages I and II', *G.E.S. Working Paper No. 60*, Department of Industry, London.

GLC (1985) *The London Industrial Strategy*, Greater London Council.

GODDARD, J. B. (1983) 'Economic Development of Older Industrial Areas: The case of the Northern Region of England', *CURDS Discussion Paper No. 53*, University of Newcastle upon Tyne.

GRANT, R. (1983) 'Appraising Selective Financial Assistance to Industry: A Review of Institutions and Methodologies in the United Kingdom, Sweden, and West Germany', *Journal of Public Policy* 3.

GREEN, A. E. (1985) 'Recent Trends in the Service Sector in Tyne and Wear and Berkshire', *CURDS Discussion Paper No. 71*, University of Newcastle upon Tyne.

HOLLEY, S. (1983) *Washington: Quicker by Quango*, Publications for Companies, Stevenage.

HMSO (1963) *The North-East: A Programme for Regional Development and Growth* (Hailsham Report), Cmnd. 2206, HMSO.

HOUSE, J. W. (1969) *Industrial Britain: The North-East*, David and Charles, Newton Abbott.

HOUSE OF COMMONS (1984) *Regional Industrial Incentives*, 21st Report of the Committee of Public Accounts, Session 1983–4, House of Commons Paper No. 378, HMSO, London.

—— (1986) *The Urban Programme*, 10th Report of the Committee of Public Accounts, Session 1985–6, House of Commons Paper No. 81, HMSO, London.

HOWL, D. (1981) 'Towards a People-based Approach to Local Economic Planning', in

P. Wilmers and B. Bourdillon (eds.), *Managing the Local Economy: Planning for Employment and Economic Development*, Royal Town Planning Institute, London.

HUDSON, R. (1985) 'The Paradoxes of State Intervention: The Impact of Nationalised Industry Policies and Regional Policy on Employment in the Northern Region in the Post-War period', in R. A. Chapman (ed.), *Public Policy Studies: The North-East of England*, Edinburgh University Press.

JURUE (1981) *Assessing the Cost-Effectiveness of Local Economic Initiatives*, Joint Unit for Research on the Urban Environment, Birmingham.

—— (1986a) *Evaluation of Environmental Projects Funded under the Urban Programme*, Report by the Joint Unit for Research on the Urban Environment, Birmingham, for D.o.E.'s Inner Cities Research Programme.

—— (1986b) *Assessment of the Employment Effects of Economic Development Projects funded under the Urban Programme*, Report by the Joint Unit for Research on the Urban Environment, Birmingham, for D.o.E.'s Inner Cities Research Programme.

LAMBERT, J. (1983) 'Clothing Industry Scheme: An Assessment of the Effects of Selective Assistance under the Industry Act 1972', *G.E.S. Working Paper No. 61*, Department of Trade and Industry, London.

LAWLESS, P. (1981) *Britain's Inner Cities: Problems and Policies*, Harper and Row, New York.

LEVER, W. and MOORE, C. (1986) *The City in Transition: Policies and Agencies for the Economic Regeneration of Clydeside*, Clarendon Press, Oxford.

MCCORD, N. (1979) *North-East England: The Region's Development 1760–1960*, Batsford, London.

MCDOWALL, S. and BEGG, H. (1981) 'Industrial Performance and Prospects in Areas Affected by Oil Development', Scottish Economic Planning Department, Economics and Statistics Unit.

MACKAY, R. R. and THOMSON, L. (1979) 'Important Trends in Regional Policy and Regional Employment: A Modified Interpretation', *Scottish Journal of Political Economy*, 26.

MANNERS, G., KEEBLE, D., RODGERS B., and WARREN, K. (1972) *Regional Development in Britain*, Wiley, London.

MARQUAND, J. (1980) *Measuring the Costs and Effects of Regional Incentives*, Department of Industry, London.

MARTINOS, H. (1985) 'Workspace Development', *LEDIS Review No. 1*, The Planning Exchange, Glasgow.

MESS, H. A. (1928) *Industrial Tyneside: A Social Survey*, Ernest Benn, London.

MIDDLETON, R. (1985) 'Unemployment in the North-East During the Interwar Period', in R. A. Chapman (ed.), *Public Policy Studies: The North-East of England*, Edinburgh University Press.

MOORE, B. and RHODES, J. (1973) 'Evaluating the Effects of British Regional Economic Policy', *Economic Journal* 82, 87–110.

—— —— (1975) 'The Economic and Exchequer Implications of British Regional Economic Policy', in J. Vaisey (ed.), *Economic Sovereignty and Regional Policy*, Gil and McMillan, Dublin.

—— —— and TYLER, P. (1977) 'The Impact of Regional Policy in the 1970's', *Centre for Environmental Studies Review, No. 1.*

—— —— —— (1986) *The Effects of Government Regional Economic Policy*, HMSO, London.

MSC (1984) *Annual Report*, Manpower Services Commission, Sheffield.

—— (1986) *Corporate Plan*, Manpower Services Commission, Sheffield.

NATIONAL AUDIT OFFICE (1985) *Department of the Environment: Urban Programme*, Report by the Controller and Auditor General, HMSO, London.

—— (1986) *Department of the Environment, Scottish Office and Welsh Offrice: Enterprise Zones*, Report by the Controller and Auditor General, HMSO, London.

N.E. TRADE UNION STUDIES INFORMATION UNIT (1985) *Tyne and Wear in Crisis*, NE TUSIU, Newcastle.

NECCA (1984) *The State of the Region Report*, North of England County Councils Association.

NECCA (1986) *The State of the Region Report: Review of Change, 1977–85*, North of England County Councils Association.

NRST (1977) *Strategic Plan for the Northern Region*, Volume 2: *Economic Development Policies*, Northern Region Strategy Team, HMSO, London.

ODBER, A. J. (1965) 'Regional Policy in Great Britain', in *Area Development Policies in Britain and Countries of the Common Market*, US Department of Commerce.

PEARCE, D. W. (1983) *Cost-Benefit Analysis*, Macmillan, London.

PEPLER, G. and MACFARLANE, P. W. (1949) *North-East Area Development Plan*, Ministry of Town and Country Planning, London.

PITFIELD, D. E. (1978) 'The Quest for an Effective Regional Policy, 1934–37, *Regional Studies* 12, 429–43.

PSMRU (1985) *Five-Year Review of the Birmingham Inner City Partnership*, Report by Public Sector Management Research Unit, Aston University, for D.o.E.'s Inner Cities Research Programme.

ROBINSON, F. and SADLER, D. (1985) *Return to Consett*, BBC North-East, Newcastle.

ROGER TYM & PARTNERS (1984) *Monitoring Enterprise Zones: Year Three Report*, Department of the Environment, London, January.

ROGERS, P. and SMITH, C. (1977) 'The Local Authority's Role is Economic Development: The Tyne and Wear Act 1976', Regional Studies 11.

RTPI (1985) *How Effective is Local Economic Planning?* First Report of the Economic Development and Employment Working Party, Royal Town Planning Institute, London.

SAUS (1986) *Urban Programme and the Young Unemployed*, Report by the School for Advanced Urban Studies, Bristol University, for D.o.E.'s Inner Cities Research Programme.

SCHOFIELD. J. (1979) 'Macro Evaluations of the Impact of Regional Policy in Britain: A Review of Recent Research', *Urban Studies* 16.

SINFIELD, A. and FRASER, N. (1985) *The Real Cost of Unemployment*, BBC North-East, Newcastle.

SLOMAN, M. (1986) 'Setting up the NCB Enterprise Initiative', *Regional Studies* April 1986, 1984–7.

SMITH, I. J. (1986) 'Takeovers, Rationalisation and the Northern Region Economy', *Northern Economic Review* 12, 30–8.

SPENCER, K., TAYLOR, A., SMITH, B., MAWSON, J., FLYNN, N., and BATLEY, R. (1986) *Crisis in the Industrial Heartland: A Study of the West Midlands*, Clarendon Press, Oxford.

STOREY, D. J. (1982) *Enterpreneurship and the Small Firm*, Croom-Helm, London.

—— (1985) 'Manufacturing Employment Change in Northern England 1965–78:

The Role of Smaller Businesses' in D. J. Storey (ed.) *Small Firms in Regional Economic Development; Britain, Ireland and the United States*, Cambridge University Press.

TAYLOR, J. (1982) 'New Jobs for Old: The Case of British Steel Corporation (Industry) Limited, *Northern Economic Review* 4, August.

TOWNSEND, A. R. (1983) *The Impact of Recession*, Croom-Helm, London and Canberra.

TUROK, I. (1984) *The Impact of Urban Economic Policy in a Context of Decline: A Study of Southwark, London.* Paper presented to the ESRC Urban and Regional Economics Seminar Group, December.

TYNE & WEAR COUNTY COUNCIL (1982) *Manufacturing Employment Change in Tyne & Wear since 1965*, Tyne & Wear County Council, Department of Planning.

—— (1985a) *Structure Plan Annual Report*, Tyne & Wear County Council, Department of Planning.

—— (1985b) *Unemployment in Tyne & Wear*, Tyne & Wear County Council, Department of Planning.

—— (1986) *Manufacturing Employment Change in Tyne and Wear, 1965–1981*, Tyne & Wear County Council, Department of Planning.

WALKER, G. and ALLEN, K. (1985) *Industrial Aids in the UK, 1985: A Businessman's Guide*, Centre for the Study of Public Policy, University of Strathclyde, Glasgow.

WEEDEN, R. (1974) Regional Rates of Growth of Employment: An Analysis of Variance Treatment, National Institute of Economic and Social Research, Regional Paper 111, Cambridge University Press.

WHITTINGTON, R. (1984) 'Regional Bias in New Firm Formation', *Regional Studies* 18, 3.

WILKINSON, E. (1939) *The Town that was Murdered: The Life Story of Jarrow*, Gollancz, London.

WILLIAMS, R. (1982) 'Tyne and Wear's Industrial Improvement Areas', *Northern Economic Review* 4, August.

WILLIS, K. (1983) 'New Jobs in Urban Areas: An Evaluation of Advance Factory Building', *Local Government Studies*, March.

INDEX